Enoch and the Book of Coincidences II

Second Messiah

By
Howard Michael Riell

"Enoch and the Book of Coincidences II: Second Messiah" by Howard Michael Riell. ISBN 1-58939-879-3.

Published 2006 by Virtualbookworm.com Publishing Inc., P.O. Box 9949, College Station, TX 77842, US. ©2006, Howard Michael Riell. All rights reserved. No part of this publication may be reproduced, stored in a retrieval system, or transmitted in any form or by any means, electronic, mechanical, recording or otherwise, without the prior written permission of Howard Michael Riell.

Manufactured in the United States of America.

Prologue

It began in 1986 with a desire to learn the true nature of a relationship with a lost love.

Curiosity led me to a paranormal class near my home in Brooklyn, where I met "Rosalyn," Michele, Teresa and others. In short order the Ouija board was introduced into the small group's activities.

Within weeks my newfound friends and I were meeting informally to speak with what the others insisted were entities from another plane of existence. I remained the skeptical reporter, yet grew increasingly fascinated. I watched as things no one could have known were revealed, and events we were told would happen actually did. Supplemented by what had become a flood of coincidences in my everyday life so pronounced and consistent with the messages that only a fool could dismiss them, my belief grew.

Soon we started receiving messages saying that Rosalyn and I had been "chosen" to bring the incredible knowledge of life and death, heaven and Earth, and man and God to the world through several books that I would write — the first of which would become Enoch and the Book of Coincidences.

It soon became more than a hobby, as entities began to appear who identified themselves as figures from both the Old and New Testaments -- Aaron, Joshua, Abraham, Enoch, the historical but decidedly un-divine Jesus and Mary, and others. At other times, we conversed with what we were led to believe were angels, and experienced apocalyptic visions. And on several occasions we received messages from an entity claiming to be God Himself.

The entities speaking through the Ouija board warned Rosalyn of someone who would appear in her life soon — I called him 'Fredericke' — who had allegedly stalked her across the centuries. Incredibly, someone fitting his description had come into her life, and soon began acting in ways she found both bizarre and frightening.

As the months passed the messages remained compellingly consistent: my friends and I had been led down this path, we were told, in order to play a pivotal role in the final act of human history, a role Rosalyn and I had apparently embarked on together many lifetimes ago.

The exact nature of that role became clear only near the end of the period covered in Enoch and the Book of Coincidences, and it struck right at the very origin of the split between Judaism and Christianity. It was the revelation that, while the man known as Jesus of Nazareth was not God, the son of God, the product of a virgin birth, nor the Messiah Son of David as Christians believe, he was nonetheless

the little-known 'other' messiah mentioned in ancient Jewish legends —
the Messiah Son of Joseph, whom lore said would precede the long-
prayed-for Davidic Messiah and be killed.

Armed with this knowledge, they told us, we were to heal the two-
millennia-old rift between the faiths and reunite them once more under
the banner of the one true God, the God if Israel, before mankind faced
a final, cataclysmic war. But by the first book's conclusion many
unanswered questions remained:

How could Rosalyn and myself (known then as Aliasha and
Matthew) having been separated 2,000 years ago have changed the
course of history by preventing the advent of a so-called messianic age
(which many at that time did, indeed, feel was imminent), as we were
told?

What exactly was the mysterious revelation that our two alter egos
experienced on a lonely road nearly 20 centuries ago?

Why would God, if that's who it was, select the two of us for any
kind of faith-based mission at all, when Rosalyn was only moderately
religious and I was an outright agnostic?

And if the real, historical Jesus was the first of two prophesied
messiahs, where was the second — the true Son of David who
according to ancient legend will battle the forces of evil, usher in the
Apocalypse and ultimately help bring about man's ultimate redemption?

The final entry in Enoch and the Book of Coincidences was made
on August 10, 1987.

This book begins one day earlier.

INTRODUCTION
(From)

"You will receive our power surge. You will be encased in our covering. We will always watch over you. You are a lead. You are the final link."... (Rosalyn) went back to the board. U ARE WORTHY. U HAVE BEEN SOUGHT AND HAVE ARRIVED.
(Sept. 12, 1986)

——

Rosalyn said there was someone there. "Someone incredibly powerful, incredibly holy. Way over any of the other guides we've gotten so far." She said he was saying that I was "blessed," that I was "chosen."
(Sept. 23, 1986)

——

YOU WILL BE OUR GUIDING LIGHT TO THE WORLD. YOU WILL SET THINGS STRAIGHT. YOU WILL PREVENT DISASTER.
(Nov. 6, 1986)

——

"Is the messiah coming?"
MAKE UP YOUR DESTINY.
(Nov. 22, 1986)

——

"You were...you were not born!...You were not born... You were... sent!... to..... bring light?... during the....... the darkness to come!?" She said she saw a very bright, white light behind me, and a ray of light leading into the top of my head. Then she said she saw a man over my right shoulder. A very old man, a very holy man, with a long white beard and a robe, surrounded by light. *"He's here for you because you are very holy,"* (Magda) said. *"You are the...chosen one..."*
(Nov. 23, 1986)

——

HOWARD. YOUR STONE MUST BE ETCHED ... WE ARE WAITING FOR U. THERE ARE MANY NOW DEPENDING UPON U. U MUST FEEL THEIR PRESSURE ON U. THEY ARE SEEKING U.... FULFILL THE VISION. U ARE DRAWING CLOSER TO THE MEANING OF LIFE.... ALL THIS MATERIAL IS RAPIDLY SPRINGING AT U. U ARE ABSORBING SOME AND UNDERSTANDING SOME. ALL MUST BE CONNECTED FOR YOUR ENLIGHTENMENT. U ARE FAR MORE ADVANCED THAN U IMAGINE. U COMPLEMENT ONE ANOTHER, AND THAT IS THE ENTIRE REASON FOR THE MYSTICISM LINK TO U. U WILL BE OUR REDEEMER.
(Dec. 5, 1986)

DO NOT WORRY. JUST TRY TO FIND YOUR WAY NOW. MANY ARE BEING SENT TO GUIDE U. PLEASE TRUST THAT LOVE IS AROUND U. U ARE SPECIAL. WE HAVE WAITED FOR U.
(Dec. 16, 1986)

U ARE GREAT. U MUST KEEP SEARCHING. ALL U WILL STUDY WILL COME TOGETHER. IT WILL MAKE YOUR COUNTENANCE WONDROUS. YOUR MIND WILL ABSORB ALL. MANY WILL BE HUMBLED BEFORE U.
(Dec. 27, 1986)

U ARE LIVING A MIRACLE TOGETHER AT TIMES ... U MUST DISCOVER MANY REASONS. U WERE DESTINED TO COME NOW.
(Jan. 4, 1987)

"It's as if your arms are encircling a large group... elderly? Sickly? As if one touch of your light can instill in them... their spirit is happy, and they know they will reach peace. Your words will bring much harmony and comfort, as much heat coming from you. You will search for inner holy being, which is you. You must find him and confront him, and become one, and you know you will face the world. You may be ridiculed and criticized, but the masses will want you. They will seek you. They will know the special one."
(Jan. 9, 1987)

H: U HAVE BEEN BRILLIANT IN MANY DETAILS. ONLY A DESCENDANT COULD UNRAVEL CERTAIN TRUTHS. WE BESTOW BLESSINGS UPON U.

"Of whom am I a descendant?"

U ARE FROM HIGHEST. U BEAR STAR. U COME FROM ABRAHAM.

"Am I a descendant of David?"

THAT IS YOUR STAR.

(March 2, 1987)

———

"You are sent to open the hearts of those seeking the truth and light. They need one to lead, one they place trust and loyalty. I know you are in this divine light. You will radiate this... You are My light."

(April 15, 1987)

———

"I have a wreath of stars.... Grace is stored within you."

(May 4, 1987)

———

"You are love. You are light. You will guide many. You must bring the lost to Me. You do not understand what is within you."

(May 17, 1987)

———

Rosalyn told me she saw a young man holding a staff, walking through the desert. The further he walked, the older he seemed to be getting. She could only pick up pieces of what he was saying. *"I'm very strong. You have to learn to lead. Follow my example...You will lead well. You will take lambs and show them the way. Both will combine strength, compassion, kindness to help the souls..."*

(May 28, 1987)

———

"You are the covenant. You have a part of My light within you... Many of centuries have passed. Part of you has been through each... There is a covenant..." (June 6, 1987)

———

"You are chosen for...... been entrusted... They're all your children. They are as babes. No place to go. They'll wander till they find you."
(June 22, 1987)

———

"Howard, it is meant to be. You are following direction you are destined for. You will direct future of multitudes."
(July 3, 1987)

———

"Crown will show us how to give the strength... Howard will be called Yaweh... Howard will be named for the Kingdom of Kingdoms that he is and will be..."
(July 31, 1987)

———

And it is here, my friends, that the story must end. At least for now. What comes next, I am told, I may not yet reveal. Just as abruptly as that, it's over.

To K, M and S.
And PA.

Part One

*And it shall come to pass in the last days
that the mountain of the Lord's house shall be
established in the top of the mountains and shall
be exalted above the hills;
and all nations shall flow unto it.
And many people shall go and say, come ye, and
let us go up to the mountain of the Lord, to the
house of the God of Jacob; and he will teach us of
his ways, and we will walk in his paths: for out of
Zion shall go forth the law: and the word of the
Lord from Jerusalem.
And he shall judge among the nations, and
shall decide among many people: and they shall beat
their swords into plow shares and their spears into
pruning hooks: nations shall not lift up sword against nation,
neither shall they learn war any more.*

Isaiah 2: 2-4

August 9, 1987

Sitting with "Rosalyn" in her backyard.

She told me she'd been unable to sleep the night before, that she'd heard things as she lay in bed. She'd seen a Star of David, then heard the name 'David,' and then the words 'Son of.' She'd also heard 'all Israel... multitudes become one whole.' There was also a man with a wreath on his head, she added, who looked to be in his twenties or thirties.

"And Howard," she said, "he looked like you."

Naturally, I was intrigued. I explained to her that 'David' and 'Son of' made me think immediately of the messiah who, according to Jewish belief, will be the son (descendant) of King David. She told me she had also seen many people walking in the desert. There were mountains in the background. "They're heading somewhere, and they're supposed to become one, or a whole."

When she saw these things she felt she had to put on the Jewish Star that I had bought her. Once it was on she lay back in bed and thought of God. "I said, 'I know You're here because you have something to do with Howard ... I know that You're Howard's God.' I felt very comfortable. I must have fallen asleep. When I woke up I almost felt like I had been somewhere and didn't remember it. No lights or anything. Just thoughts being thrown around in my mind."

Rosalyn also said she had seen a large hand. She had seen something similar several weeks earlier, but now it was vertical instead of horizontal. She got the sense that it was very strong. When she got up she said she had removed the star so that her children wouldn't see it, but later felt very strongly that she had to put it back on.

"I feel very attracted to it, and I feel it's got to be on me," she said. Of the man with the wreath, she told me, "To me it was like... he was tall, he had dark hair. I can't say that it was you, but it was similar to you. I saw him in profile; he had a longer nose. I sensed he was supposed to be somebody... 'David' kept coming into my head. 'Son of ....'''

August 11, 1987

The coincidences continued. At work I had to edit an executive's title that began with the initials PA. I smiled. Eight lines below that, I found another executive named Nikodemus.

I stopped smiling.

Rosalyn called from work. She said she was ill, that she felt drugged. I urged her to go see a doctor. She called again later from home. I suggested she try automatic writing; that it might drain off some of the excess energy. She called back later and told me she'd written till she'd fallen asleep. Here's what she wrote:

Where are you going? You need only think of Me, and I am with you. I am full of love for you. You have not meditated on Me for a while. You have felt Me and have seen his (Jesus') face before you. I know you relate to his presence. It is a human form. You have work to do. Do not fret. Your partner will always be at your side. He will always sense when you need him most. It is as a fireworks display when you share yourselves. The two are one beacon. You must learn to join together and harness your thoughts. Each has much to lend to the other.

I shall forgive your being without a white veil this time, since you are experiencing physical unwellness. I shall send you light. Your partner can lay on his hands and enfill (sic) the light. He, too, will benefit by this since he will feel what he can instill in you. Please remember to hold his hands when you have gained energy and feel what is vibrant between you. You will feel the presence within you.

Do not hesitate. Give yourself completely to each other and you will gain strength to pursue all paths before you. Love is a strong ingredient, and your bond shall not be shared by any human. You will find the time to be tranquil, and you have this peace with each other. Continue to stand by him with encouragement, and be an avid listener. He is the fruit of our plan.

Later, Rosalyn said she began to pick up scraps of words:

You are My choice ..... You will always be in the light .... have been given physical form to feel what they feel .... You are My liaison ..... The words you are penning are inadvertently scripture ...... You are one with My prophets. I do not wish to be angry with you, but you must separate .... Thou are in My hand ..... I will try and instill .... in you. You must learn to accept it. ... Great energy flows through him to you.

I wish to speak to you further. Energy is radiating from every part of his body. You will feel .... from the darkness ..... no other two have been placed .... keeping you in your physical form to experience and feel what they feel. Light comes over his shoulder and into you. You are encased in light.'

Later on, Rosalyn got still more:

I am very pleased when you write. I see every letter. I sense every emotion ... I am in every word .... Use this energy wisely. Many will be strong interfering with you. They sense your strength individually. Together you are ...... Do not let them divert you. You are truly a master (at solving puzzles, she thought). Find the correct passage. They will have the answer you are looking for.

Rosalyn also saw a ladder in her mind's eye, and heard:

You are advancing. Whatever he requests you must give him. You are walking to Me. You will eventually be in the center of the light. You are My liaison. What one gives to the other is returned. You are confused. If I were to give you the answer your shell could not (accept) this light ..... You are tied to them.

August 12, 1987

At Rosalyn's house. She began to write again:

Upon your higher soul. Meet challenge. Demands are made on you. Sought out. Not looking for that wreath I told you about. See it - no man.

"Who is it?" I asked.

To all.

Rosalyn continued to write:

I want .... heed my words .... law...

I asked once again who the man in the wreath was. By now Rosalyn was speaking, not writing.

"*Do not be so eager. Do not rush what must be slowly put into you.*"

"Yes, but who was it?" I insisted.

"*Why are you antagonizing? You have shown you will have great love. You have much that will be imparted. The vision was fleeting glimpse.*"

"Of whom?"

"*You are in ... you must help Me .... one sends prayer. One has reached Me.*

"*You need the one ..... had ..... please speak the words. Please send Me, reach Me ... your prayer .... please pray ....*"

Just then Rosalyn seemed to get excited. Something was wrong. I tried to wake her up, but couldn't. She spoke again:

"*I am ... I am ... I have to step back. I have to come back now.*"

I calmed Rosalyn down as she came to. When she was all the way back she told me she'd seen a man in front of her. "It was somebody bad trying to stop me, trying to come through. They sensed where I was. Some kind of face. It was trying to block what I was feeling. They didn't want me to connect with anything, to see something."

August 14, 1987

On the phone with Rosalyn.

She was sensing a presence. I told her to ask about the man with the wreath. She said:

"When I think about that man I have to be very still and very meditative. I'm seeing myself. I don't know where I am. I can't see you, but I feel you holding my hand.

"I can see almost a shadow of this person, the one with the wreath. It's not like I saw it before. It's only a shadow. He's so strange... like I've got to really be able to concentrate. I'm holding onto your hand. It's almost as if I can see two different things. I can feel you, but I can't see you. But I can see him, but not feel him. I see him from a side view."

"Ask him to turn around," I said.

"I'm missing something," she said. "I'm hearing, 'I'm not ready.' I think he's got black on. It's almost as if he's trying to say, 'You're not prepared, you're not ready.'"

"Tell him Howard Riell asked you to ask him to turn around and look at you," I said.

"Come with her."

"How?"

"As if you're coming right inside of me."

"Why don't you tell us your name there, my friend?" I continued.

"Now, think of me and find the right words."

"How can I do that if I don't know your name?"

Rosalyn started to hear a word like Masala. "Do you mean messiah?" I asked.

Rosalyn spelled it M-A-S-S-A-L-A. Then a moment later said, "No, you're not ....."

"Not what?" I asked.

"On the last step."

"Why does Rosalyn see you and think of me?"

Rosalyn interrupted. "Howard, I can't do this like this. You have to be with me. He's not saying anything. It's almost as if, the way I see you in me, you're now going into him. I keep thinking of him as you. I feel like I'm being put on the top of a mountain peak. I can't. I have to hold on."

Hoping that he was still out there somewhere, I asked, "What do you have to do with the Son of David?"

Rosalyn said she heard a word that sounded like "*'Incarnate.'* He's pulling you. You're not quite into him. Some part of you is not quite into him."

"What is he ashamed of?" I asked, losing patience.

"He's not here yet," she said. "I don't understand, I can't ...."

As usual I went too far. "In that case, then why the cheap theatrics?" I demanded.

"You will .... hostile .... you are incomplete ... you are not .... you must become ready ...."

"For what?"

There was no answer, but Rosalyn looked at me and said, "You can't put this in the book (my first, which I was then working on). I don't know why I'm saying it, but you can't. This is being given ... and this is a higher elevation, and this is not .... It's something very different. I feel too displaced. Like I'm in two places, and I feel like I'm dealing with two of you. Like I'm in two worlds. Don't make me do this, cause I don't know where it's going.

"Howard," she continued, "I have this feeling of being very close to you. I'm drifting too much. I can't ..... I'd like to know who this guy is. He's you. I can't help it, he's you. How can there be two of you? I can't take two of you. *I can't handle one!"*

August 15, 1987

At Michele's with Rosalyn and Teresa.

Rosalyn went out like a light and began speaking:

"All must shed mortal emotions. You must put them away. Pull over you cloak of cleansing. You must be one unit. If you concentrate on the energy level around you, you will feel strong presence surrounding you. Here are all highly tuned to us this time. She is shedding any impurities to stand in this light. You all can sense at least part of our flow. You must leave the problems behind. You must concentrate only on feeling our presence. There is white and there is purple. Four are to be encircled. There is deeper message, what seems to be above me. It is deemed for just two. It is much higher than what I can deliver this night.

"I wish to be present when the two receive message, but I will not have the privilege. I may only continue with this circle. It is warming to have been permitted to see the two will become. There is much I will deliver to you. I may only speak to the four. What is deemed for the two I may not remain. You may not receive this this session, but I am not certain of when they will deliver it to you. You, the four, must close circle."

We all held hands and the session went on. After a while, however, the speaker returned to the message that was just for the two, which we assumed meant Rosalyn and me.

"Two need to be special conscience of the added energy instilled. They take advantage of this. Their special mission. I lead the four. You are love. Extending ability when concentrated is like lightning exiting. I wish for you to be in tune. I wish for you to truly take advantage of our light. It is not given often. It is not given unwisely. It is not given unless proper channels are open."

A little while later, Rosalyn got a word she said sounded like 'hamalach.' I recognized it as meaning "the angel" in Hebrew. I asked what the special meaning was.

"I am here to lead you on a path. You have already begun this journey. I will return to the two when they are prepared for me. I am simply showing you there is more to come when you are prepared for me. I shall be forerunner. The two of you must be meditative and cleansed before you call on us. The next time together you will have to bear the all. You will have settled to room you prepare. Much presence builds up waiting your approach."

Rosalyn finally came out of it, but told us she was hearing the words *'Saint Joseph,'* and *'take away the sins of the world.'* She evidently had a lot of energy going through her, and she picked up a pen and began to write:

I have put words into your mind. You are relaying my wishes. Great prophet will be revealed. Open up your senses and you shall hear my message.

We continued a short while later when Rosalyn again lapsed into a trance. The speaker said she and I were "branches" of the same tree:

"The life force must run through both. I will give you the data you need. You are both part of Me. The tree .... I illuminate ..... You were attached to My light. You are an extension of My ..... tree will expand far. You will gain much knowledge. Your strength ... will make the two ....."

"What can you tell us about the man in the wreath?" I asked.

"He will be as your shadow."

"Who is he?"

"He is not ready to be revealed. He is coming too slowly."

"Is he the Son of David?"

"Yes."

"Why does Rosalyn sense a connection between him and me?"

"For he will work through you."

"In what way?"

"He will .... My ways shall not be questioned. Some other of your ..... I choose to appear in many guises. Accept .... no conditions. Many were called, not many were able ..... I will be fair and .... the tree is .... to overlook no head cover (my head was bare, as usual), but it is ... life force from Me to you to her. You can ... You will be ready for what I will tell you. She will think ... and you should be full the next joining with her think of My awesome ... You must both be in proper .... I have filled you. You must join your minds. You will be as one thought. The tree limbs will have the same vein. Your own veins will ....."

August 16, 1987

With Rosalyn in her backyard on a beautiful summer night.

Rosalyn said she saw four men who "will ready you, train you. They'll work with you, talk with you. I see them as people. I don't see them as guides. They are guides, in human form, to ensure that you will learn what you are supposed to learn. It's almost like you go to a special place to be with them."

Rosalyn said she got the sense that I'll be locked away for days at a time studying at some point. "They are to tighten you up. When you're with them you're in a special place, a special building, a secret place. They are there to teach you."

What they will teach me, she said, was not psychic in nature, but rather something I must be prepared to do; to face people, to deal with them. "When you walk away from them," she said "you are to be completely prepared." I asked jokingly whether or not she sensed that I was married.

"I almost feel as if you can't be," she said, "otherwise you couldn't devote the time you need to. These four are very secretive. No one knows about them. They will come to you from very ordinary circumstances."

I asked her what exactly they were preparing me for. "To do verbal battle," she said. "You'll be reinforced. I don't see you sitting in front of books. Reinforced in your beliefs, in the history of your people. You will need to be alone much of the time because what you will have to face .... You may have to travel a lot. If you had a family you couldn't. You may not marry until you're older."

She also started to see the two of us walking alone by the sea at night. "I think you have a yarmulka on," she said. "It's almost like I've got something similar on my head. I don't think it's here. It might be in Israel."

She started to feel a presence from under the water and said it was "like we've been told to come to this spot." I asked her with whom I would have to verbally battle.

"With those who will not accept. I'm getting, 'the anti-Christ,' but it doesn't fit it. To counter his lies? Versions? Beliefs?"

I asked whether he and I would meet face to face. She answered immediately. "Yes."

"On television?" I asked.

"No, you will have some words privately, just the two of you. There will be one other person from both sides with you. The two of you could never really be alone."

She saw the two of us in what she took to be a hotel suite. "I'm holding on to you, but I'm not there," she said. "I'm confident nothing can happen to you, yet I'm worried."

Rosalyn said she saw me hugging her and saying, 'I'm confident; don't be upset.' I asked whether or not I would realize that this was the so-called anti-Christ when I met him. She said, "You'll know beforehand who he really is. This is part of what the four were training you for; like, by now you both have become noted, you both know you're vying against each other. Your feeling is, 'Why don't we meet and just be face to face?

"He's very smug," she continued, "and you're very confident. Like, your thinking, 'I can knock him right on his ass.' It's like you're someone special now, it's as if you have to put on a certain front for people, yet you and I have not changed. He's going to say something like, 'So, we finally meet.' He's older than you; not old, but older than you."

She described him as having some gray hair, good looking, and a leader of something, like an emissary. "He knows who he is, and he knows that you know. You're acting like two gentlemen. It's as if it's kicking off a battle."

I asked Rosalyn, "But doesn't he know good will ultimately triumph?"

"He doesn't believe that," she said. "He very much thinks he can defeat you. It's not going to be easy, Howard."

Rosalyn also told me that she saw a man with long hair and a beard. She saw him telling me after that meeting, "'You've done well this round, my son.' This person hovers around you," Rosalyn told me, "but with that meeting the gauntlet's been thrown down."

I asked, "But who am I to be meeting with the leader of a country?"

"Your claim to fame is that people have been coming to you," she said. "You're loved by people and you're against anything he's for. Almost like two politicians campaigning, but for souls instead of votes."

She said she could also sense him thinking, "'You've been a thorn in my side.'" She also said that by this time I will have had several books published.

August 17, 1987

Reading the front page of the New York Times.

Lots of noise recently about something called "harmonic convergence." People held hands at sunrise all around the world yesterday to help usher in some kind of New Age that will save the world from disaster, as prophesied by several ancient civilizations.

Hmmm. It is happening at just the same time that all of this messiah stuff is coming through. If the messiah business is true, then harmonic convergence — especially the timing of it -- might also be true.

That night, I was on the phone with Rosalyn.

We had been talking about the man in the wreath. She slipped off into a trance after a few minutes:

"Am I him?" I asked.

"You are one in him, or vice a versa. You are one in your Creator."

The trance didn't last long, which was fine with me since I had no idea what she was talking about. She came out of it a moment later.

August 18, 1987

Somewhere around 3 am, asleep in bed.

I woke with the sound of my own name echoing in my ears. I waited, then again, like a flood, it came. I realized what was happening, and I listened.

Although no further words came through, I seemed to remember that I had been dreaming of writing. I remembered it very clearly. It struck me that I had been writing names from the New Testament on a piece of paper, possibly with a quill. Could it be that someone woke me so early in the morning just so I would remember that?

Later, at Teresa's house with Rosalyn and Michele, Rosalyn went under quickly. Here is what she said:

"You must feel words. You will hear them. You will sense message within you. You will be able to connect with the words. You may get a few at a time. You may not receive it all in one day. Will begin to flow. What you get do not discard. What you receive another day will interconnect. You also will recall slowly what's given to you in sleep."

I asked whether I could assume that what we had been getting lately was beyond the bounds of my still-expanding book, Enoch and the Book of Coincidences; whether from here on in anything we got should not be placed in the book.

"Correct. Great energy is filling. Sit, meditate and write. At times you will meditate together. Some words may flow easily that way. Try to have a candle lit when you write. Many of your words will be inspired. Do not abandon confidence now. Do not permit her to retreat. She has much enlightenment to assist you with. You are as opening from a cocoon. She sees emanating from you. It is powerful. Messages meant to lead proper course. Words are as fire. You will be very alert to what is transmitted through you. Do not hesitate to reach one another. Sometimes (when) you are receiving something you will both need to draw energy from the other. If this occurs do not hesitate at any time. The other will need to sense it. Write proper names in the book. Keep the book beside your paper. It will lead to assist you in receiving messages. Candle I hold is to help lead you."

"May I ask your name?" I asked.

"I am not in cape (Rosalyn had sensed someone in a cape earlier). *I am in prayer. I hold candle to lead you. I am your… Who can you most shake her with?"*

I knew the answer immediately because ever since Rosalyn had come up with his name out of thin air I'd been able to blow her mind just by mentioning it. "Are you my great-grandfather, Aryeh Lieb?"

"I will give you some light that will help you see."

"Do you see much that I can't see?" I asked.

"Yes."

"Do you see the guy with the wreath on his head?"

"Do not cause me to have to leave you." Apparently, there were rules he had to follow, and one of them was not to reveal anything to us.

"Sorry," I said.

"With lightheartedness that this is permitted I am condoning you, I am blessing you. And the respect is noted."

I asked whether I could ask another question.

"You are insatiably inquisitive."

"All I'm asking is who spoke to me last night."

"Will be shown to you. Do not disappoint me." With that, Rosalyn leaned forward and kissed me on the head. *"I, also, not expected to come this time. Your appetite is strong. The flow is right, and she received it. Be careful. Be aware, too. Will be even more attuned.*

Some will be spontaneous. The energy seems to shoot from both. It can be given and received. Have picture of me."

I asked where a picture of him could be found.

"Probably buried in box."

"At my parents' house?"

"No. Try to at least visualize me and let mine be one of the names you ...... Hashem is with you."

August 19, 1987

Back in Rosalyn's backyard.

She was picking up vibrations again. She saw me as a teenager. There was something hovering around me, some sort of light, and she got the sense that it was there because I was too young. She heard the words:

"Until he is ready... he doesn't see us ...."

Rosalyn also sensed me hovering above crystal clear blue water. She heard:

"You must be completely cleansed in the crystal water. You are coming of age. You are now beginning to be satisfied."

A little while later she sensed that her deceased father was nearby, and seemed to hear: *"You, who believe this* (all the psychic stuff, I supposed), *now can't accept your own father? You can't talk to me, so I'm going upstairs with your mother."*

After a brief rest Rosalyn once again began to pick up messages. She sensed an authority figure, someone special and holy. She started to whisper:

"You must be very aware."

"Aware of what?" I asked.

"For looking within yourself. Much will be cognizant."

"What will I find?"

"That which you shall truly signal. It is as if you must reach within your heart and soul and then pull out what is deep inside you."

I asked who this was.

"I have sat with you many occasions." I immediately thought of Philo. *"I relished the love between you. Many enjoyable hours were spent. I loved you both as my own. I am now being privileged to... hopefully see the wheels I helped put in motion spin this lifetime. Do not lose what you have found. Do not let strength slip from your fingers. If the two need to hold to the other, there shall be complete confidence. You are finding your inner soul. You are feeling self, but you must complete the test deigned and destined. Do not be lackadaisical. You are to be the vessel to reach many."*

"Why have we been getting this entire gang from the year 1 A.D., with yourself and Jesus and Matthew and Aliasha and Nikodemus?" I asked. "Why them? Why all of you?"

"Because we should not have been rejected. It is now as the seam that is split, which must be sewn and sealed together. As strong as she is in her faith, you are strong in your beliefs. You have learned to be open to her feelings, and what has been placed before you. As she struggles with her beliefs she also feels she believes in your faith. It is of higher importance in this age that the Jews and the gentiles unite. They will need the strength of forces."

I asked whether or not Jesus would somehow serve as the bridge with which we would close the chasm between the two faiths.

"Yes. They must be able to harmonize. They must join forces, for a greater threat will lay before them."

I asked whether or not the Jews would have to accept Jesus as a prophet.

"More than prophet."

I asked whether Jesus was in fact the first Messiah, the Son of Joseph.

"The first house."

"Is that a yes?" I asked.

"Yes."

"And what of the house of David," I asked.

"It is being readied." I asked him to explain. *"Only one is permitted to speak of it. It is not I."*

"I've been led to believe," I said, "that he has something to do with me."

"I am here this night because of the way I could calm you when you sat with me. You must try to be patient. But you must try to allow the awakenings to come slowly. You must ..... each happening, and I know you have always been analytical. I feel that you must wait, for it is only He who chooses the time and place, and you must not assume. You must have Abraham and/or Aharon bless you with a visit at least once before you will receive some answer. Do not give in to becoming rambunctious. I am pleading with you. You are dealing with what you are beginning to feel spiritually and in a physical sense. You are dealing with her spirituality and sensitivity, and you must consider both. You are very, very close. You must not overlook any feelings, dreams, thoughts that you feel."

I asked PA whether my book would bridge the gap between Jews and Christians.

"It will take much more."

"Will it take an apparent miracle?" I asked.

Rosalyn smiled. *"It is, but I am sure, as usual, you will be in the front of things."*

I asked whether the Lubavitcher Rebbe, Menachem Mendel Schneerson, knew that the messiah was preparing to descend to earth.

"Not presently."

Thinking back to a session long ago, I asked PA whether Bressen was really his brother.

"I shall have to admit to him."

I asked whether or not we would find Bressen's name in any book about Philo of Alexandria.

"Possibly one, but it was very vague."

A short time later PA prepared to depart, and he told us, *"I wish to stay with you. I know I must depart. I very much wanted Aliasha to come out now. Could not be handled this time. Want you to remain in the right path. I do not wish you to separate. A complete unit again. Must never happen. I feel I may return at least once when she .... she worries and watches for you. I know you feel protective. Sometimes you seal your strength and bond. Is necessary. I do not have the right, but I still extend blessings and wishes. Good bye both of you."*

Before he left I asked whether or not he felt the prayer that I offered concerning him and all others who have come to Rosalyn and me to teach us.

"I have recognition of that. It is only great part of me can come to you. Believe that your prayer is very powerful."

I asked whether another part of my morning prayers -- in which I ask God to bless the souls of the victims of the Holocaust -- is also felt.

"He may answer you, but I know the light has entered that darkness because of you."

"Why must their pain continue so many years after the fact?"

"You must see future. Be satisfied to know that you have brought light and do not question His ways. Much pain has been overcome."

"Is it wrong for man to question His ways?"

"I do always admire that in you. As much as there were times I tried to knock it out, that is what has brought you to this end. Just be careful how far you question."

I thought back to that episode a couple of months before in which Rosalyn laughed at the end of a session and was about to be punished -- and then when I laughed during a session the very next night, and was also about to be punished. I asked why God was so quick to anger.

"You must await until you will come before Him. But I do wish you to know you must be aware of anger when shown case of it.... that many have mourned other times. You are so very, very blessed, and the love that is surrounding you is wondrous. Do not forego what has been placed encircling the two of you. There is much love to be shared. There is much that has not unfolded. Do not ......"

"But why is He so unforgiving?"

"Were you unforgiven? Did He lock you away from her? It was very close, but so much is expected. So much surrounding you. Do not lose sight of the fact that you both need ..... to ...... surround you ....."

He was gone.

Read.

It is said that the Messiah, Son of David, will arise from the lowest, the most base elements of humanity. This derives from the idea that the messiah will need to attract all the world's people. He must draw followers from the lowest and the highest echelons of society, not merely the scholars, or the righteous, or the devout. Thus, it is said the messiah will come from the lowest. Of him it is also said:

* The messiah will come "in a generation fit for extinction..."

* Just before the messiah's advent, "insolence will increase and honor dwindle ... the government will turn to heresy ... academies will become bawdy houses .... scholarship will degenerate. Piety will be scorned. Truth will cease. Youths will be impudent .... and a man's enemies will be the members of his own household."

* "Do not imagine," Moses Maimonides wrote, "that King Messiah will perform signs and wonders ... revive the dead or do similar things. It is not so."

* "If there arise a King from the House of David who ... observes the precepts ... prevails upon Israel to walk in the way of the Torah ... and fights the battles of the Lord, it may be assumed he is the messiah. If he does these things and succeeds, rebuilds the sanctuary on its site, and gathers the dispersed of Israel, he is beyond all doubt the messiah. He will prepare the whole world to serve the Lord with one accord."

August 21, 1987

At my apartment. Rosalyn speaking:

"I bestow blessing upon you, my son. You are bringing her into the faith. It is meant that she be a part of you. She must also share in your dedication. She should be part of this heritage. She once was. One was very strong faith. It is as leaves falling upon you both. These leaves bring insight, perseverance, reinforcement, a new opening. They are falling all about you. They are covering you. They are a symbol of something to be formed.

"There are many lined up this night. There is a white door that is opened. Hold fast to one another, for you may never experience the hierarchy who may appear this night ever again. It is meant to be a celebration, and the two of you will learn to celebrate completely with one another. She......"

Rosalyn said she sensed a woman. *"Do you not remember me? I stood by the well with you many times. You even offered to fill my.... with water."* By the well? Miriam? I wondered.

Suddenly, there was an orb of light, Rosalyn said, and people in front of it. There was a man with a long beard. "I've seen him before.

He's over your head. A ceremony, some kind of ritual... his hands... It's right that you have this on," she said, touching my tallis (prayer shawl). "His hands are above your head."

I asked if he was holding oil in his hand (it made sense in the context of what we'd been getting). She nodded. "Is he anointing me with oil?" She nodded quickly and emphatically. I seemed to feel something pushing my head down. Rosalyn sniffed, and said she smelled incense. Was Aharon near?

"Do not face me. You have advanced exceedingly since my presence. It does justice that the head is covered. I still wish to communicate with you. When her visions manifest I can feel her strongly. When I wish to speak with you I still look upon her as a woman, but I can sense the link, and He has still not chosen to have you completely feel yourself. Do not discourage, for there is a reason.

"I have given you strength. You have a strong road before you. I may never speak with you again. That shall be decided in the future, but too much is blossoming around you. I am very strong for her, and your always remaining on this plane gives her the balance necessary. Many houses around you. When one has been selected, it is with a great deal of courage, fortitude, strong religious conviction. You will meet this path that is being opened ahead of you. You must commune in your mind and your soul with Him. You must feel the amber light flowing into you. Joshua was sent to you. Joshua will defend you. Joshua will appear. He should arrive this convening, yet... if he.... cannot lose her... Put the star in her hand." I did. "If he does not arrive, he will next session. He must. You should realize I am an omen."

"Of what?"

"Of what still awaits you. I bring holiness and prepare sanctuary. It is not trivial. You have opened yourselves to what is destined. You still.... you need guidance and direction, but you have found many answers, many times without much assistance. He has chosen well. I ask that you at least occasionally have incense burning for me."

I said that I would, then asked if I could sense my son.

"I will give you a sentiment this night, only I will give you to know that I was very much around you when you said those prayers (in naming the boy). *He is in a light. He was sensed when she walked in. He will have a touch of a hand upon his head. You are the one who is having the flow enter him. I am only lending assistance. His soul is tied to you. There was much love sent out from you, and that she was present, it also circled him. There is no malice within her heart, and this child, between the two of you, was billowed in the rays. I must not deviate. I am here, as you were told. I want you to understand. We do not always not adhere to what is told you. I know there have been disappointments. You have weathered many in the past. You have overcome many doubts.*

"You have a strong strength of purpose, which you may still need to instill within her. She does not have that incentive. I fear she only lends herself because she knows it is necessary for you. She must learn to also give over. The two of you are very strong. You must have the purpose of reaching the top of the beam. You will go through many phases. You have understood many of the visions she has told you. She has seen the holiness."

Suddenly Rosalyn buckled over, apparently in pain.

"I.... will be departing soon. I wish for you to continue the sojourn. Many who have bestowed blessing upon you are surrounding you this night. If you.." More pain. *"....if you deem she cannot go on, please try to continue again. Try not to lose what is surely circling this night. They will not leave, so do not fear that if you stop they will also depart. They will not leave this night until the two of you separate. You are truly one. As Joshua was given commands to lead, you must take up and venture. You may be mocked. What did you think when first I appeared to you? You would have known as much now. You are chosen. You must accept. You all would wail if such planning was rejected.*

"I am out of character, as you would say. But I do wish to return. I feel the love within your hearts, even if she has not been in the temple. You have been placed together by Him with special care. He is a loving God. He is a righteous God, and much must be lived through. The world has made a mess of itself. Please remember: if you end, please pray, and when you reopen, pray. Your prayers are very powerful. I am going to call you my son this night. As you have placed your son to me (I had named the baby in spirit Aharon) *I shall never abandon you.*

"(I) feel your words within me as I have not felt words spoken in ages. They are sincere, and bond of respect is between us. I must pull away, for I came too soon. But what is abounding this night is so strong I could not resist. I truly do not wish to inflict physical feeling in her, but she is very negative and I am very overpowering. I extend apologies. I truly bless you both, and I cherish what you have spoken to me."

Rosalyn came slowly out of it. After some conversation, she asked me who Jacob's son was. I told her it was Joseph. Interesting that she should ask that, since the whole concept of Jesus being the Messiah Son of Joseph was so integral a part of what we had been getting.

She started to throw words out. "The first of a line? Something passed on? Two lines..... is destined for the following generation...." Before I knew it, she was out again.

"You are at correct threshold. He was begotten of my son. David's house is present. Different from first. Times are strange. Help must be given. Here your lineage is strong. Never have I so spoken. There are many stars twinkling this night. As my son knew his fate, so you are foreseeing a life awaiting you. There are times which will be lonely. You will feel as if you are the only man on this earth. There are times when many will be supporting you. Accept their wishes. My son was not...

some of his strength and... will be offered to you. You will have choice accepting it or not.

"You are very open-minded in certain areas. You will have... to open. You will be shocked to see how much flows. You will stand near the sea and you will reflect and you will feel one with those that have felt His presence. Your mind must be clear. My house is large. Must unify the houses."

I asked whether I was speaking with Joseph of the New Testament.

"I am begot of my father Jacob. I am......You have my only..." Could this be Joseph? But which one? And what possible connection could there be between the two of them?

"I do not chastise that there is a star around her with my symbol around her neck. I was as you at my youth. I was your age. Many things hurt. I suffered much for what I tried to bring about."

There was a long silence, punctuated by some incoherent murmurs. Finally:

"You will feel much. You will have mental vision. You have strong background. .. You must accept what you're seeing and feeling, you love me....You must place some of that love into him. He has much to face. I will be near him through most. There will be many decisions to be made. There will be much opposition. Do not worry. But you are doubting your beliefs. I know how strong you are to me. You will find the bond to his beliefs. His are not so different.

"Much of what caused church should never have come about. You may find that you must go over to him. If you do, he will help you. Begin to place your trust in him. Lend him all your insight, and all your spiritual and physical... for he must want to face.... of his. He is the last. He will always wear crown.

"You have much, before you. I was her savior; as a brethren to you (was this supposed to be... Jesus... we were listening to?). *With my strength to you, my power I would place at your disposal. I know how much you are feeling, and how much you will feel. I give you the first gift... Do not hurt her. She will be also shaken in her beliefs. Be gentle and kind. I wish to keep her love and her trust and faith in me. But if you choose to want them with you, I am relinquishing, for she has much to give you, and I must dwell in past. The gift is great* (that) *I give to you. Between you is even greater. There is so much that has been placed between you.*

"You have been told not to ask of the wreath. I was as one intruding this session. But her faith in me is strong, and you are showing that respect. You have no concept of the great eyes watching over you now. It is a rare, rare occurrence. Your future is... unchangeable."

I asked what the connection was between himself and Joseph of the Old Testament.

"I feel the one spoke to you now was Joseph's. I was Nazarene. I came from his light. There was much confusion over my birth. I once told you, I consider you a brother. Know the truth. This is part for two only (to) *be able to know. You will have the answers, and if you have questions they will always be removed. I am going to... I bow to those in the wings, for they are greater than I. I worry for her. I place her in your hands. I say shalom."*

"Shalom to you," I answered.

After a while my arm began to hurt. Words formed. I dictated to Rosalyn:

"There are giant words that must be spoken. Many lives hang on a thread. Many will be saved. Many will open their hearts to you. The two are gleaming examples."

That was apparently all I had to say, because then Rosalyn started again:

"The children will be joyous first. Much love emanating from you. Much compassion to be delivered. How do you think the messiah will be recognized? The trees are full of.... but some there will be bare. Just as the animals store for the winter, you must store much of your knowledge. What is being given to you is in reserve, and you should know the empty time to fall back upon it. The proper time will come. As you built a foundation, so do others begin their craftiness. You (shall) *speak with me."*

I... I... Why are people so tormented? Why are they turned so from the Lord?"

Rosalyn said she saw a vast expanse of sand. "I'm seeing, 'The sons of Israel.' Not old men. Wandering; having wandered; will wander. One son of each tribe? All unity? Reuniting?

"It is within your right hand I place strength. There is much healing in your fingers. There is great light comes through you. Red is the heat. Cleanse your eyes with cold water. Cleanse your fingertips. Cleanse your ears. You are very precious to me."

"*It's all light coming from you*," Rosalyn said. "*It's stemming from inside you. Must.... so as to receive. Must... it's goodness; it's all goodness. It's all miracles. It's all healing. It's within you...... I am within you. I wish...you must listen to the...You must learn what is yours to hear... Be very strong. Do not be misled by someone who may enter your life. They will seem very prophetic. Be very careful. Do not fall into traps. Open yourself to Me. Become My light. It is so strong. Never permit darkness to prevent the light from coming through. May you feel Me... Your senses will know I am within you.*

"There are so many that want to speak with you. My son, many kisses are upon your head this night. Much healing has been placed within you. My light is within your heart. My light will stay within you. You will know the time to open it, and when. Do not be misguided by false people. I have told you, you will need to depend on each other.

There may be times when you will truly need the reinforcement from each other, for many false situations may be placed before you... You will stand within that temple one day, and many learned men will listen to your words."

"The great temple in Jerusalem?" I asked.

"Yes."

I asked if I could ask about the messiah.

"You are permitted to ask. I may have to give you a riddle. So much is in confusion, but you are owed the right to ask."

I asked whether, as we'd been told, I was, indeed...... him.

"You are a messenger. You are sent from Me. There are many problems in your time. You are now in a form. You may not see some (sum?) for many years. Yet you must know what is being given to you, for there are many you have aided just from this knowledge. My son:Truth that emanates from your lips will reach so many. You will never know the number you've reached. You..... I don't know how long she will last."

Rosalyn did, in fact, seem quite uncomfortable.

"You may need to return (as) I am speaking to you... Although I am speaking to you, others will have messages to help you. Need to get through. I give you the enlightenment to (save?) many souls. You must have the tongue of fire. You will know who should be reprimanded obediently. You must receive... You are to be splendid. You will have My words, and they will be on your lips. You will know what to speak. You will distinguish what is inspired. You will never lose sight of the role you are... Never lose sight that I am within you. I love both of you.... with many, many blessings."

Rosalyn seemed to come partially out of it, and said she could see the Ark of the Covenant. Moments later she faded once more.

She could see it while He spoke. *"Be quite aware of the covenant. It shall be unearthed in your time. You will stand on a spot where you will sense it so vividly. It needs to be before you so you can feel the strength of your purpose."*

I asked whoever this was why I'd had such a horrible time on my trip to Israel back in 1983. It had really been a gruesome trip, so rotten I'd vowed never to go back.

"You could not (stand to) see the luxury and the exploitation of that state. What you saw was correct. You must return when many things have been connected with you, and look to connect with your past. You and she have been locked for a reason..... started those times in that place, and you will open more at that time....."

Rosalyn awoke, and it was over. Long night.

August 23, 1987

On the phone with Rosalyn.

She said she could see Aharon at an altar with two men beside him in golden robes. Someone's telling her to "*let loose what's behind*" her eyes. "*You began there; you must end in same heritage. Let golden light come in.*" Next, she told me she saw a man holding two tablets (Moses?). "*You will be wise.*'" She said she sensed the Ark, and heard, "*It will give you strength.*"

There was also something about "*Opening up... only the right....*" Rosalyn said she saw me opening it. "*Only the right one can open it up. When the right one was in front of it and opened it...*"

"Who is the right one?" I asked.

Rosalyn said, "I was seeing you standing there." She also heard, "*I will bring you to the spot.*" It was, she said, the scene she'd seen before, by some sea.

August 28, 1987

At Michele's with Teresa and Rosalyn.

Late in the evening, Teresa began to slip into a trance. She said she could see a man atop a mountain with his arms held out, holding a quill pen and a gold book.

"*I return to let the archangel read the gold pages. I am shining the light upon the cap on my head that I've worn many times. Center warmth at the opening, through golden book. I would give knowledge supposed to be given. He will receive the light around gold book* (the Book of Raziel, which is published with a shiny gold cover). *Doves will appear around him. He knows the white doves of his teaching. I come through him. You don't know him yet. Not to be told until two become one. Thou shall be thy truth. Two doves of white are they, to hold the gold ribbon with the open book. I am mighty to them* (Rosalyn and me?) *in meaning. They know what I'm saying. Through you I come to let them know. Soon, two of you will be informed. Soon, when they will reveal themselves. Give them time to read the messages between the two. Open gold book; read messages supposed to be given. It will only make sense to them.*

"*One will receive the coming of me. One will know when I am to be seen. This is special tonight, as a blessing, for thee who knows me will understand. Follow the blue light two of you hold. Each will give together as one bond of ribbon. Time will bless the event. Use your prayers to feel the message between. It must come from the unknown that knows nothing of passages. Two are trying to receive. You soon will give it to one who keeps it sacred. Thou shall reunite and rejoice with the two. Chapels in background will pray for this new occasion. It will be seen between two of you. I stand in center holding gold book. It is your strength to be used. I bless the event coming to all. Two must feel it first to give it out. They've been at one time there. Band of gold will connect around blue lady and man in white robe has to wear the scarf. Scarf will give energy through gold book. Clear water must be around each other. One white candle in center. Two lights will appear on candle, which will be seen in eyes of blue lady and white robe. This will show your strength through the coming of me."*

We wondered afterward if this could have been the entity we'd been referring to as "Mr. Wreath." If it was, how could Teresa have known anything about it? Rosalyn and I had never mentioned a word of it to her. Puzzling.

August 25, 1987

Alone at home.

No sooner did I lie down in bed then I felt like I had to write. I grabbed paper and pen and waited.

My child.

There is too much to hope for. You can still make any decision you want. It is an opening for you. You may paint the picture as you see it. (I had been wondering whether or not I was supposed to use any of the messages that came since the end of my last book in its as-yet-unwritten conclusion.)

The words of hope are as candles in the wilderness. They light the way. They can still now turn back. Many thrust forward into the abyss. Gentiles, Christians are doomed to discern their transgressions. They will pay them back. More than one will heal his pain. They will make adjustments to their faith. No room for doubt. It is like a tent. It covers the whole congregation, yet it provides shade from weathering forces.

There is too much nonsense. Too many joyful when work is to be done. Attractiveness is belying hard truth. My Chosen People, too, have strayed from My path. They have done abominations in the name of survival when it was not necessary. I asked whether that referred to assimilation.

Yes. They can now go forward and stand behind you. You will redeem them. They will look to you as a master. The gentiles will look to you as a savior. You will deliver them, and bring bread before them. They will eat of it and they will know they have lived in a shadow. They will thank you one day, when their pain subsides. None will oppose you when finished.

Many are the times you have wondered if you are the messiah. I can say that you now are he who will deliver his people to Me. You will clear them of their sins. You will give them clean breath. They will swarm around you and cling to your arms. They will love you, but first they will suspect you. They will not think you are who they say you are. They will have to be shown. They will be shown. It is incredible, the light you will bring them, and they will know you are he whom I have promised.

Nowhere does a plan exist to wrangle the truth from his lips (I knew this was a reference to the so-called anti-messiah, who is, by the way, mentioned in Jewish lore). *He is as a deceitful snake. He is the viper. No good will come of anything he says. He will spit upon them, and they will take it for rain. You will meet him face to face and joust with him. He will seek to return, but they will do as you ask, and he will be returned.*

Stay not the ruin of the land. It will be burnt and cindered. The ground will fall upon the ground. All shall see ruin. All will feel the pain. He will tremble the world. They will smoke and blow bubbles and whisper and sleep.

I suddenly saw a young man with dark hair and a beard, wearing a plain garment and a blue robe, or sash, slung loosely around his shoulders. He seemed to be slowly gliding upward, looking down at me but away, as if I were standing to my left. I knew that he was saying goodbye for Him; that I had done well in receiving the message.

I was only minimally aware of what I had written because I had been so intent on keeping my mind blank, so as not to influence the message. When I read through it I was dumbfounded. I read it again. I decided to call Rosalyn, but first I read it a third time.

Any doubts I'd had about the genuineness of the message left quickly. These were not my words. I knew that. They had come from someone else.

August 29, 1987

At my apartment with Rosalyn.

She began speaking.

"You are receiving our words. You will act upon our words. You will feel them. Will be embedded upon your soul. I travel from great distance to reach you. Never discredit anything you receive. Remember the place I first made contact. You will be at that spot soon. Make me proud, and you will show me great honor by your deeds. Think of me for a few moments when you are in that house."

"I don't even know who you are," I said. Rosalyn smiled.

"I did not realize I was such a riddle. I said it would help you. You have a special... other garb, other than just the proper hat."

Now it was my turn to smile. It was my great-grandfather, Aryeh Leib Kabakoff. He had once reminded me that I was wearing the wrong hat (a cowboy hat) while speaking with him. It had become sort of a standing joke. I also knew the house to which he referred: my parents', where we'd first made contact. I welcomed him.

"Has been long since I have permitted myself a smile or a laugh."

"Why is that?"

"Ohhh, serious business. None of religious studies should be taken lightly, but you have gotten so deep. You, so to speak, have come through the back door."

I couldn't help but be touched by how true his words were. Any normal Jew is taught the basics of the faith as a child, and perhaps one day may (age 40 is the norm) reach a point where he can begin to study its mystical aspects. Yet here was I, delving into enough mysticism to choke a horse (so to speak) and only now beginning to learn a scant few of the basics of the faith. Back door, indeed.

"*But I am proud, so proud. Instead of frowning, for once, I will take the chance. It's easy. I find your little friend (Rosalyn) pleasant. It is so calming to come through. You have made good choice. Connection is always proper. Connection will remain because you both give. Never lose that respect. You may grow even closer. Do not worry. I will take care of anyone who does not like it. You must concentrate on your writing. They are sending many vibrations to you. I do not even belong in this league.*"

"Don't be modest," I said.

"*I feel very happy this night. It is difficult. I wish to speak Hebrew. It would not come through easy for her, and you would have hard time with it. Never disregard a thought or feeling you receive. You, hopefully, are... You will see me more. The two of you (are) like exposed wires, and when you touch they can sense the explosion. So many. You have managed to even bring me closer to another realization.*"

"What's that?" I asked.

"*That I will be permitted to..... into you, so that you will be the word that is received to many hearts.*"

Rosalyn covered her face with her hands and seemed suddenly uncomfortable.

"*Oh... although the agony burns in every Jew.....*"

"Are you all right?"

"*I have tried to turn my thoughts away. I came in light-hearted, and I wish to leave the same.*"

It dawned on me then what had happened. I had been about to ask about the Holocaust; at least, I had *thought* about asking. But I hadn't said anything. Apparently the thought was strong enough to be sensed by my great-grandfather -- and to cause him discomfort. I regretted having thought of it. It appeared to have had hurt him.

"*I did not mean for her to sense. She is not indifferent. She feels just as strongly. Tries not to think of it. It is deep in you.*"

"From your perspective," I asked, "why was it (the Holocaust) necessary?"

"*I..... do not comprehend the suffering. We must know it has been unending. My hope is... you may be the culmination... I will try to return later. Please concentrate upon me this week.*"

Rosalyn came out of it quickly. We took a break. Soon, she said she was seeing Mr. Wreath, the one she'd said she thought was me. He was part of a procession; there were lots of people in front of him.

"I still say he's you," she insisted. "But he's a little different. He's thinner; his nose is different." She covered her head with a shawl, was silent for a moment, and began to speak more slowly.

"*We have told you, you will blend. You must have your eyes open to see what is before you. Heed that we explain cautiousness.*"

"Who are you?"

"*I play many roles. I... sands burn easily. There is great peace there. Stands wholly round. He has not come full circle, as you have not completed circle from one direction to the other. Will join proper moment.*"

If this fellow with the wreath and I are to join and somehow become one, I asked, which of us will be the dominant personality? Will Howard Riell have to disappear?

"*Do not worry. All attributes will fall into place. You are the physical manifestation.*"

I asked when all this joining was supposed to happen.

"*I'd venture six months. Checked all factors. They are deciding on when and who will come in; if they shall appear.*"

"What happened to the first messiah, the Son of Joseph?"

"*I am not to give you your answer. I will say I hope they come this night. It is clear and it is open, and I feel you shall ask your questions if they permit; if they decide to face this. I am glad I am at least once permitted to herald their coming. I know I want to see you accomplish the call. Cleanse selves and pray. When you return, have a prayer and ask if they will permit your speaking with them.*"

Rosalyn's left hand twisted into a claw. She grabbed a pen and wrote.

"*Do you not see that you are walking endlessly through the desert? I have been over you for many centuries. The people have been subjugated for their.....*"

Rosalyn began to speak once more. "*Many were led into battle. Many were called to serve. Was great suffering. The (ravages?) of man and God. Perhaps the time has arrived to battle minds... Cover your heads. Do you not see the smoke, the great mist, that soon will engulf you (the Shekinah? God's presence?). As Joshua led armies, you will lead different armies. You will penetrate where they do not realize you are entering. You will blend the knowledge. Your people will be not like everyone else..... Will enter their minds. They will plant the seeds. People will know the true path to follow. Much tension will arise. The masses will be frightened of destruction. This planet will come close to its annihilation. Such fools.*

"*I place the staff within your hand. Your left will hold it, your right will lead. Your right will direct. One has passed through. He recruited many. He was not the true, no... It is true, he suffered much (referring to Jesus?). It had to be done; a first, to pave the way. A test was given. You must stand among the correct group (undoubtedly directed at Rosalyn, and referring to the Jews). You must return to your heritage. There was a reason for you to assume the role. Someone had to experience the feeling for him in order to understand the...... Do not be frightened of the mist. It is the camouflage. Behold what will come to you.*

"*I have sent My people always. I reiterate that the first has been here. The second must succeed. Do you know who stands here this night? If you... You have circle. You have Abraham. You have Benjamin. You have Moses.*"

"Do you have a message?"

"Aaron. I am... My son, this world can be harsh and cruel at times. Your heart must be seen. You must have love, compassion; feel weight of God. You must write the proper words. You will know how to put all accumulated. I said I would give her strength. I will stand and put that strength inside.

"*He* (Aaron, I supposed*) is preparing incense. I stand between the two of you. I have My left on her, and My right on you.*" The speaker (Speaker?) said something about having to make a choice.

"I'm fighting with myself," Rosalyn said. "Part of me is holding onto Christ."

She paused, then began to speak again.

"*She must dare it. She... let it run cycle, and then you must give her back........*"

Then:

".........Matthew, I think I'm lost. I feel like I'm in darkness."

Suddenly it was Aliasha! Judging by what I could tell, I wasn't simply looking in on her life, 2,000 years earlier. She appeared to be speaking with me in real time, communicating with me directly -- across time itself!

"I'm not Matthew," I said.

"You're not, I know, Matthew, yet you somehow, you're Matthew. I don't understand. I am between where............" I called her name.

"You were lost. I know it's you..."

I spoke her name again. "Aliasha?"

"Yes."

"It's me."

"I feel like I'm between two places. I'm not me. Matthew!?"

"Aliasha."

"Yes?"

"Where's Philo?"

"I'm frightened."

"Don't be. You're all right."

"Matthew, you're the only thing that's familiar."

"Don't be afraid. I'm with you."

"You look different."

"Still handsome, no?" I said to break the tension.

"Yes."

"Thank you. I'm glad we've established that." I urged her not to be afraid, but rather to "be thankful that we've been allowed to come together again."

"I don't understand, Matthew. I'm not me. I'm within someone else."

"Human bodies are just garments we wear and discard," I told her.

"But we're different," she said.

"No we're not." I asked, "Who separated us?"

"They're looking for us. We have to..."

"Do you know Bressen?" (PA's brother, who told us he'd loved Aliasha after she and Matthew had been split up).

"Why are you asking this? Why, Matthew? PA is with me. He's always... Philo's always helped us."

"Did I finish writing his book?"

"No. No. Do understand? It's like I can look back, Matthew."

"Do you remember when we were on the road and we saw the prophet?"

"Of course."

"What happened?"

"You know what happened."

"Tell me if you remember."

"There, this place. So much to look into it. We enjoyed listening to him. We used to spend... If you're Matthew, you remember. We used to spend so many afternoons just listening to the prophet. Sometimes sitting in front of his house (Philo's?). And then sometimes go to this grove, and we'd just lay on the grass together."

"And what eventually happened to the prophet?"

Her expression turned dour. "They were so cruel."

"Where was he buried?"

"The day was so dark..."

"You stood at the foot of the cross (as a matter of fact, a pair of psychics, years apart, had told Rosalyn just that)."

Her voice was growing weaker. "Matthew..."

"Why did they say afterward that he had been resurrected?"

"Some woman said that it was open, and they saw him. And you know the men who followed, the ones that were close to you. They began preaching.... You have to know this."

"Did he really rise from the dead?"

"I believed it. I missed you then."

"And what happened to Mary?"

"She... went with one of them. She was... she was so kind. She reached out to me. She told me I would find you some day. I didn't believe her."

"Now you know she was telling the truth."

"I always completely trusted you. You know that even when I placed my love in you, and trusted you, somehow we knew that the marriage wouldn't happen. That's why we gave so completely. I will always trust you."

I asked about the man who separated us.

"He didn't care about him. He sent you to that place."

I asked what happened to Philo.

"He moved." She said something about an incident with Philo when "we saw two others before us and we didn't fully understand." Interesting. Did Philo, whom history tells us was a mystic, somehow give the two of them a glimpse of... Rosalyn and me?

"I'm ashamed to tell you I became angry at God. Confused. I felt like God abandoned me, and we got in trouble for listening to the other one. I loved his mother. I wandered. I became pretty much of a loner. Oh, Matthew." She added later that she wandered "because I hated him (Fredericke, Rosalyn's nemesis, as he was back then) and she (Mary?) hated the way he could manipulate us."

I mentioned that Rosalyn has two daughters in this life. "Are they yours?" she asked immediately. When I told her no she became visibly downhearted. I told her that in my time there were those who believed that Jesus was actually God Himself. She corrected me by saying that that was what many believed in her time, too.

Our conversation went on for another half hour at least. It was as natural and clear as if she was actually here, sitting beside me. In fact, the conversation flowed so naturally I couldn't write fast enough to record it, so I stopped altogether.

I recalled that she laughed in disbelief when I told her of machines that could fly in the air ("Oh, Matthew, *birds* fly!").

I told her that people rode in those machines from one place to another. "But how can they see where they're going?"

I told her about telephones. "For instance, if you were in Alexandria and I was in Jerusalem, I could talk to you."

I asked if she knew what language she was speaking ("It's complicated. It sounds funny."). When I told her it was called English she repeated the word slowly ("Eeeeeeengliiiishhhhh????").

I got complete disbelief when I told her men had walked on the moon ("Oh, Matthew!!",) but she added that "we used to (gaze at it) often.").

I told her I lived in a country that was not even discovered in her day. "*Is this* where they have the machines that fly?" She was happy to hear that her friend Philo's works were still being read. She asked if we still saw and talked with him. "Yes." "Has he changed?" "No," I assured her, "he hasn't."

She asked if I was still shy, and ventured, "I can tell you're close to God. From the way you talk, you must be very wise." I also remember her lamenting, "So many people didn't talk to us because we listened to him."

I asked her what the so-called Revelation was. "We saw two people we thought were us in the future." (So, I thought, I was right in supposing that that was what it was!) Finally, she simply said, "I'm spinning," and she was gone. Rosalyn came to briefly, then laid back and fell asleep.

By now it was dawn. I locked the apartment door and walked the few blocks to the beach. There was a warm gentle wind, and the sun, just beginning to rise over the houses of Manhattan Beach, shone bright red. The water rushed over my sneakers as I stared into the face of the new day.

Love. Aliasha had loved Matthew. And God loved Aliasha, and took pity on her loneliness, and so he had given her some last moments with him. For love.

God had swept aside Einstein and all the laws of time and space. For love's sake he had worked a miracle, had set aside time, so that his beloved daughter could once again laugh with her Matthew.

My eyes moistened. I thought of Andrea, and of love, and of God's infinite, incalculable mercy.

August 31, 1987

At my parents' apartment with Rosalyn.

"Most Jewish girls wore coverings. I know, you are thinking you are not a girl; you are a woman. You're still young enough to be called a girl. Would you give me the respect of covering your head?" Rosalyn sensed my great-grandfather. She put her white shawl on.

"*You are still studying. Soon you would open your own bookstore. Thank you for the babushka* (the Russian word for a shawl; my great-grandfather did, after all, come from Russia). *Although I enjoy seeing you playing... with one another, I am not lighthearted. I am glad that you believed my words. You did come with the intent of contacting me. I am here because I instructed that I would be at this place. I should not have doubted that you would have adhered to what I said. I am finding difficulty communicating. Do not abandon my request, please. If I cannot get through I apologize, but if you find it in your heart to seek me again I hope strength will have increased. I am being called. Someone is ill.*"

Indeed, my beloved aunt Molly, my mother's sister -- his granddaughter -- lay sick and dying in a hospital bed.

"*Much strength has been given. She is weak. I want to be by you. I want to instill the proper choices in you. You have unraveled many confusing data placed before you. I want you to hear me inside of you. When you sit and you read begin to write something; picture me standing at your side. Feel the rabbis' encouragement. Remember the holiday, the holy day soon to come. If you can explain it in some way, share it with your friend. It is important that she see what understanding true meaning for the day is.*"

"You, I put great blessings upon, if I may be allowed to do that. I again apologize that I am being drawn someplace else. I vow to you that, whenever possible, if you call upon me, I will try to be there, and I beseech you to please return. I will be with you. I am very strong this week around you. I do not wish to lose that, but she who is drawing me... He feels I must go to be by her bed."

"Is it her time?"

"I am trying to prevent it."

But why, I wanted to ask. My poor aunt was suffering greatly. Wouldn't the merciful thing be to remove her from her withered body and bring her to everlasting peace?

Too late. He was gone.

September 1, 1987

At Rosalyn's.

I asked her to psychometrize (sense the vibrations from) a note with the words 'Super-Secret Organization' on it.

It had been my theory from the very first mention of all the messiah stuff that there had to be, *had to be*, some group of mystics somewhere who knew that the messiah had arrived on Earth, and had set up some sort of covert apparatus to find/ inculcate/ educate/ finance/ protect him once he realized who he was.

Rosalyn saw me sitting in front of a rabbi, writing feverishly on a yellow legal pad. "You must combine two lives," she said. "You are learning... to be prepared for something."

She saw the name Metatron, indicating "*strength within you. You found your link. You will need much assistance... and you will need to pick a few extremely close confidants, and also friends. You will need their encouragement, and to have them as an outlet to listen to you for yourself. They will be willing to be near you when you need them. You won't be in contact for a couple of years with the right...*"

She said she saw the letters M-E-S-S-I-A-H, "like each letter is on fire. Like it's written in flame. Do you expect something on a silver platter, or should I say a gold platter?"

Rosalyn said she saw me standing before a long table with men sitting around it. "They're asking you questions. Something's being put on you; it's white with gold in it, over your head, like a poncho. They're talking Hebrew or Yiddish. You're standing at a pulpit, reading from a book. There are a lot of old men sitting there.

"*Be ready for the coming of the one we all wait for. You're so eager, you're so avid. It has always been the fate of your people. Things never move rapidly. We are concerned with the suffering... Do not give in to your great youthful exuberance, though we do not wish to see you lose it, either. I do not understand myself why scheme must be drawn out. Perhaps your quick mind has absorbed so much of this...*

such a huge puzzle you have pieced together. You know that you come out on top... apex is yours...

"*You, Son of David, will be crowned, for you are reaching... More of this lifetime is so great, as a magnetism you exude. Are many (on) this Earth that will support you. There are as many souls who will lend energy. The suffering will have served a purpose. Rejoicing will be great at the final moment.*"

Rosalyn said she could see "gold, like a chariot. Lions? Angels, all angels, the sky is full of angels. It's you, it's like, almost like you're untouchable. There's a very strong feeling emanating from you, like, when we talk about... it's God. That kind of feeling. Almost like an unseen force."

September 2, 1987

I woke with the words, '*Their disadvantage is they don't know you're a messenger of God*' echoing in my head.

Rosalyn called me at my office. Last night she'd had a flash or something about Aliasha. She was riding in a caravan and apparently passed right by Matthew without knowing it. "They never knew that they were that close."

September 6, 1987

Around 7:15 a.m., alone in my bedroom.

I had lit a yartzeit (memorial) candle the night before for my father's father, and prayed fervently over it. I opened my eyes in the darkened bedroom and turned toward my dresser, where the glass-enclosed candle stood.

Flame was shooting ferociously out of it, close to a foot into the air. I was galvanized. Without taking my eyes off of it I reached over and grabbed my glasses and put them on. Violent tongues of flame were leaping out of the glass. I sat up and stared, holding my blanket over my face in case the glass should explode out at me from the heat.

Minutes later the stalks of fire fell, and the flame went out, replaced by thick curls of black smoke. Stunned, I knew that this had not been an ordinary event. I wondered whether someone was trying to send a message through. I picked up a pen and pad and waited to see if any words came through. They did.

'*We want to show you the force of your prayers. They are strong, like a flame. All-consuming is the fire within your veins. No one does with you as he pleases. (Henceforth) we will guard you and run ahead of you, clearing a path through the briars* (I could vaguely see some sort of forest in front of me). *You command the fire; your words have fire in them. Direct it at your enemies and they shall be warned* (next, I saw a ball of flame). *Your flow of energy is constant. Your amazement is nearing its end. Divided in your line* (the line of David?), *the veins carry forward through the generations and reunite at the appointed place and time.*

Faculties can sense that you are especially aglow. The measure of a man is his glow; like a fire at night amid the wilderness the Earth has become. It is you who will redeem that fire. Rest assured (now I was seeing several Biblically-dressed men) *that when you really start getting our sensations this is when it will be* (meaning in the early morning?). *Good morrow to you, and God bless you.*

September 9, 1987

Rosalyn and I were both getting messages. I couldn't understand hers. Mine were unmistakable.

Failsafe... missiles... underground explosion... pressure build-up... massacre... millions will run... the ground will shake... zone... bomber... skyrocket... amazement at such widespread death... so much death... cool wind, cold sweat... ! will/must turn my eyes away in tears... ! will hear the cries of my (My?) children, but I will not/cannot look upon it... My messengers of death will seek out My children and catch up with them... the guts of the Earth will vomit up... wind-wracked... kingblast...

Rosalyn started writing with her eyes closed.

You are of one line. The two of you are the same... I feel, like, a big heaviness, Howard. Someone very laden down. Like all gold on them. Very serious. Very.... regal? A ruler, I think."

She stopped talking, and was silent for many moments. Then:

"*I do not make appearances. I do not want the star* (of David) *brought down. I became destructive. I wiped the slate. Many were slain. I do not communicate. I do not choose to participate. However, you are heading in my direction. I will meet you there some day."* I asked for a name, and she started drawing.

"... Lion... my herald... not destroy as I did... descendants... discover my blood, which lines bring out... The true leaders stand on a throne and command respect from their people. Force is necessary to overcome enemies. Israel... For some reason you must also attempt to save gentiles. I can see her beside one she had great faith in (Jesus, no doubt) *beside the Son of David. Her only true heritage -- only a Jew is all feeling with their God -- and her seed is from the same...*

"Come to the covenant and stand in their light. She will wear the veil, also. All her powers and she does not truly comprehend. All of them will be at your disposal. She will be able to tell you what lies before you and which course to follow. Your dreams will also give you answers.... You shall become the savior for those who believe in the anti-Christ and the true messiah of the chosen people.

"The two of you are bringing in great rabbis and....... The light does shine within her. Have too much to absorb and realign in what I feel is a doomed world. He wishes you to save them from themselves..."

Several points in this monologue hinted it might have been King David himself speaking. Rosalyn took the ring bearing the Star of David off my right hand. Moments later, she spoke.

"*Beautiful piece of light. I do not wish for you to feel all this turmoil. You deserve to also feel serenity. There is enough that lies before you. You deserve a respite. The burden is too much to speak of anymore this night. Peace will be upon you both. I will not tax you physically. You do have physical responsibilities.*

"*I am anxious. I await your being before Me and asking for Me. I am in your midst, and I will come to you when you are truly before Me as one again. Remember the love between you. Remember how much love I place upon you. I even overlook the coverings* (on both of our heads which, oops!, were missing) *for this night. I did not even plan to interfere with you.*

"*David always* (faced?) *the unknown. I do like having come through tonight. I do not... I am determined I will not give you so many messages, so I shall stop. I am anticipating you.*

"*I am your God. I am guiding you. I am patient, and must wait till you.... of accepting. I will speak to you soon. Then the reverence and the true preparedness must be present. I do place a light within you. That light shines to others. They may not know what it is, but they feel it. The light that is in you now will shine and glow. You must learn what lies before you. You* (are upon?) *Earth to also bestow blessing.*

"*I must depart, for I almost became human, and am enveloped in the emotion and the innocence and purity I feel inside.*"

The logical conclusion? The first speaker seemed to have been King David; then, perhaps, someone else, and then, well...

The part at the end ("*for I almost became human*") troubled me. I can only assume it meant that He was allowing Himself to empathize more strongly with our emotions than even He wanted to. This is not unprecedented; at times throughout the Bible as well as the midrash (oral legends), God does say that He regrets His own reactions.

September 11, 1987

At my place.

"*You are as the sun that brightens the day,*" said Rosalyn, in a trance, "*so you brighten life. Book* (Enoch and the Book of Coincidences) *is first accomplishment in steps up the ladder. Your insight will become even more acute. Do not doubt that you are to record what is happening. Your words will become permanent.*"

Rosalyn started trying to mouth some words that sounded very much like Hebrew.

"*You will enhance your abilities to comprehend. You will accept what is being sent to you. You will endure whatever is necessary to keep the people together.*

"Your words mean much to Me. Your heart is open. Never hesitate to be weary in front of Me, to let your burdens be expounded to Me. Much is laden upon your shoulders. I shall never cease to be at your side. Adhere (to) My commandments.

"Adhere... what is in your heart. When you celebrate this new year, there is much to look back upon, and use this to look forward. The future is...must be expanded.

"The light which surrounds you cannot be absorbed completely. To explain it would take lifetimes. You must not overburden the human aspect, which must function. You must make the contact which is inevitable. You are the favored. You will spread the word. You will receive many whose pleas may seem intolerable. You will often feel (you) do not wish to cope with all that is placed before you... You must set apart, and only those of utmost importance. Must be distinguished, for much will be before you as none in the past have had to deal with.

"Wreath of gold above you. Each step brings it closer to setting upon you. I do all things. I can stop this world. I can wreak havoc. I can place love. You have been given free will. Whatever destruction and chaos befalls man is brought by him. Everything shall take its course, and that is why I do not completely interfere. You have found this path through each other, and through your own cleverness. You have come to Me because your light is strong. My love is always within you...

"I wish to bestow kiss upon your head. You will also receive My energy through you. Take rest. I promise you I am not departing. I never leave you, as you prefer, spiritually. I know there is weakness presently. Let a respite. I am overpowering this visit. Do as I say. Find some way to reinforce her... she is not holding on. I will not interfere physically, and I know the energy is very high this night. Messages must go to you."

"May I suggest," I said, "that You send Your message through me instead of Rosalyn?"

"Must concentrate. You still need My... You will (be) almost as the Bible says of Adam and Eve -- made of one (I would realize only many months later how significant that last statement was). *And as she is gifted, she receives flow from you. She receives much input from within you. You are a conduit...*

"You will be the leader. You will take charge and know what to do with information. You will place order in all the chaos. Accept your roles. You still need part of her. She cannot give that now... Your paths are not the same as hers, as she, of course, does not have what you were tested for. When you wish to try, she will know what to do."

When Rosalyn came out of it she said she could see "twinkling stars," as well as "two very large angels, almost standing guard."

My suggestion evidently carried some weight. After relaxing with pizza and TV, a message did, indeed, begin to come through me.

I saw neatly dressed college students and knew that, whether they were Jewish or not, they were studying the Torah. I saw a bright, beautiful Washington Square Park in Manhattan. Youngsters were walking around enjoying a beautiful sunny day, and I knew that they knew God. I mean, I felt like all of them, everyone, *knew God firsthand.*

"When the messiah comes,"I related to Rosalyn, "everyone will be filled with the knowledge of God."

I suddenly realized that I was seeing the world in the future, in the age of the messiah, after the wars and the carnage. It was all fresh again, sparkling clean, right down to people's souls.

I knew that in the time I was viewing religion had transcended mere religious bounds; studying the word of God was now a basic, a fundamental part of even "secular" life, because everyone was now "hooked in" to the cosmic consciousness. I   thought of the prophet Isaiah's description of the messianic age: *"The world shall be full of knowledge of the Lord as the waters cover the sea."*

Hadn't I had that vision way back in the beginning, at Michele's house (recounted in Enoch and the Book of Coincidences), of an amber light encasing the entire globe; of the light filling men's heads and creating what could be called a universal consciousness? What I was seeing now must be the result.

"God has gone mainstream," I remember joking.

I was looking at a young, neatly dressed student sitting on a bench in the park. It was as if I could see inside his mind, as if there were a flickering candle inside his skull. "It's the spark of God that now burns within everyone," I said.

I could see inside the kid's chest, into his internal organs. They were saturated with the same amber light. I could picture him or anyone else for that matter walking down the street and simply deciding to stop, kneel down on the sidewalk and pray, to commune with God, and no one thinking there was anything the least bit unusual about it. I started to hear words.

"Throne. My crown. Will help you find your place, your path to the glory. I am master of thy fate. You will rise before Me and you will fall at My feet. You will begin to understand penitence. My shadow falls upon the land. My grace will fly from view. Destruction wholly dispersed."

Next, I felt an overpowering heaviness descend upon me. I lifted myself off the chair and slumped down onto my bed. I felt Rosalyn sit beside me. There were long moments when I tried and could not lift my head up off the mattress. I closed my eyes and felt like I was beginning to drift off.

Then it happened.

For a split second there was a light -- as if someone had cracked open a door no more than a hair's width and closed it again. *But the light!* There was an ecstatic exultation, as if it had enervated my very soul. Words fail miserably to describe it.

Then it was gone, and I relaxed.

I realized what it was from my readings. Somehow I knew, *knew*, that I had just seen the Infinite Light. The "*Ein Sof Ohr*," as the Jewish mystics called it. The primary emanation of God at his most infinite. The highest concentration, the highest frequency, if you will, of God. It had lifted my soul as a wave would gently lift, then lower someone floating on water.

Yet, a moment later I found myself growing angry. Was that all, I wondered? That most fleeting wink-of-the-eye? *Was that all I was to get?* It had been over before I knew what was happening. I felt embarrassed to ask, but I did. Like Oliver Twist. 'Please sir, may I have some more?'

What happened next I was only vaguely aware of; as if I was viewing it from a distance. As if it were happening to someone else who just happened to be in my body.

The "door" cracked again, and this time the light hit with force.

I felt my soul fly up, wrenched out of me.

I exploded, and was carried away like a rag doll in a raging sea storm.

My body spasmed; I flipped over on my side, my arms and legs contorting about me.

I heard the words, "*Oh God!!*" and realized a second later that they had come from my own mouth. I endured a fleeting sense of shame for having shouted out so in front of Rosalyn.

My body trembled in the greatest, most all-consuming, most vicious ecstasy I could imagine. I knew in that brief moment, knew without even having to think about it, that I was totally, totally at His mercy.

Then the door closed, and I collapsed once more.

My body became like lead. For many minutes I laid still, not thinking but not asleep, either. Then the blanket was lifted, and I sat groggily up.

I know now why the Bible says that no man may look upon the face of God and live. I had glimpsed perhaps a second's worth of the most infinitesimal fraction of His radiance, and it had sent me spinning out of my head.

Even now, when I think of that night, my insides leap. My soul, it remembers. And I will remember forever the night I gazed straight into the face of God.

Part Two

"The Fifth House, through which Gihon flows,
is built of silver, crystal, pure gold, and glass.
Its beams and gold and silver, and the fragrance of
Lebanon pervades every hall. Here I saw silver and
golden couches, sweet spices, with red and purple
cloths woven by Eve; also scarlet yarn
and goat's hair braided by angels;
And here dwell the Messiah, Son of David, and Elijah.
When the Messiah asked me: 'How do the Children of Israel
spend their time in the world whence you come?' I replied: 'In
hourly preparation for your coming.'
At this, he wept."

Rabbi Yehoshua ben Levi

September 12, 1987

At Teresa's with the whole gang.

Rosalyn began writing.

H: You will need to be your brother's keeper. Your leadership will be sought and advice requested soon. It will show you that people shall be drawn to your peace. Ye shall have the patience when required for those most in need. I see you teaching -- dressed all in white...

I should say at this point that Rosalyn and I had said nothing of all this messiah business to the others.

How, by the way, did I feel about being told that I was the messiah?

Like I should be flogged.

September 16, 1987

On the phone with Rosalyn.

I'd instructed her to write down and then psychometrize this phrase: *'They know you're here; they're waiting for you to come to them; they will recognize you.'*

She said she saw old men with beards and yarmulkas; 12 of them, sitting around a large table. A pile of papers sat before each one.

"They're reading," she said. "Someone causing a disruption. Something not the norm. Someone -- some kind of teaching. Like, 'Who is this person? What's he trying to do?' I have to assume it's you."

"You mean they're reading my book?" I asked.

"Uh-huh," she responded. "They're not angry, just discussing. Like they're saying, *'We can have answers for so many documents, yet we can't come to an answer on this.'* They're thinking so hard, arguing with themselves. One person is saying, *'He's touched it; he's touched upon it.'* They're wondering, *'Why did you start this? Delved into all these secrets?'* I keep getting one person saying, *'He is right, you know he's right.'*"

Rosalyn started automatic-writing, reading it to me as she went.

Our house is in yours. Sense our impulses. You have related much. Do not falter now. The major task is still before you.

"What's that?" I asked.

Where do your priorities remain? We are not to be placed on a waiting list.

"Who are you?"

We precede holy ones. Remember, there is a heavy burden before you.

"What, specifically?"

Leadership of the tribes, of all believers. Will search you out... You will eventually be center of many actions.

"Why do you refer to it as a burden?" I asked. "It sounds to me like a great blessing."

Do you think an easy task? It is not. A great deal of research involved. Much patience and knowledge... Reliance upon her insight will sustain you. Many blessings are to be placed upon you to fortify your mission.

"Is anyone looking for me now?" I asked.

There are some who believe he is here. I will come when proper moment arrives to connect with them. Trust in yourself and believe in her instincts. Your visions will clear. Puzzles will disappear.

I asked if there anything physically wrong with me, referring to some sort of minor urinary tract infection I had.

Do you wish to have yourself unclean? You are to become holy....... You must be cleansed. You cling to worldly feelings... Human feelings are involved. You must think... before any involvement. You do not want your physical capacity decreased because you are being groomed for, as you would understand, a holy coming. Many await you. Many do not believe you will come. There is much you..... but some of it must be..... slowly. Be more mindful of who you are becoming.... no one has lived this........

Rosalyn awoke on the other end of the phone, and I put my pen down.

September 18, 1987

Rosalyn, Teresa, Michele, Raymond and I had had a long, emotionally grueling session at Teresa's house. When it was done Rosalyn I drove back to my house because she felt there was a message that had to come through for me. We started at 3:40 am.

"I'm getting, *'Your words must be preserved. Generations... it will be inspired..... You have completed much. You relate the words we give to you... You have tied many loose ends. You have seen hidden meanings. Have been many obstacles, yet you managed to... There is much pride from all..... Don't you know what is truly inside you? Don't you know... is of divine inspiration? It will never cease to flow through you... You have not accomplished all. You are just touching the outside... There were a few chosen, are a few so extremely high... As you hear, you will speak, you will write.*

"'*There is much suffering. There will be much suffering. You will know that these must happen. Do not question why, just know that it is..... There will be much placed within your mind and within your heart. There will be many, many who will not know where to turn. You will be the only one who can lead... You will not wait a year to write the second* (book -- and I didn't, either). *You will feel us within you. You will know it is constant. So many people will be touched by your words. Many will purchase when cannot truly afford to..."*

Rosalyn faded, then came around. She said she was feeling another presence. I asked who was there.

"*Hanoch* (my Hebrew name, whose anglicized form is Enoch), *you will complete the task others have tried to accomplish.*"

"You mean writing this book (Enoch and the Book of Coincidences)?"

"*That is just a step, a very strong, strong beginning. So much in your life that is filled with God's love, including the book. You are receiving much light. You are receiving much knowledge. Do you accept that God is within you? Do you accept to complete His task? You have accepted many statements. Now being requested to accomplish many. You will be the one who will face all the obstacles. You will make decisions. You will advise.....*

"*Beware of the very, very serious complication in the future. There will be lives you are responsible for. You will be a man, and expected to help conduct yourself as such. You will physically appear as I am. You, your soul, which already is part of me.*

"*So many names, so many centuries, so much wilderness. You felt frustrated. I would also. You have risen above so many things. You have risen beyond* (what) *most could comprehend. I do want you to write, for you must give the words to many.*

"*When battle comes, you will have to meet faces of several... Angels will be sent to encircle about you. You should sense some of them... This is a special gift to you, because you have been so diligent and avid in the work which has been given to you.*

"*I am very happy and pleased with My son. I use that term; she is relating this, and will relate to that. I am very happy.... My instrument* (Rosalyn) *appears very weak this night. I know you will have perfect finished copy of the book* (Enoch and the Book of Coincidences) *which must be published. You know this was only leading you to what lays before you. So clear... Many have come to you. Remember that all who give you any message stem from Me.*

"*I am all omni*(present?). *Nothing, none would have transpired if not permitted by Me. It is a slow, tedious process at times. Have strength in your faith. For a while, you must deal with the way. Accept.... will come when will be recognized for who you are.*"

Suspecting now that this was, indeed... God... with whom I spoke, I asked whether there was any prayer I could utter that would convince Him to end, or at least ease, my aunt Molly's suffering in the hospital.

"*Your body is a vessel that holds your soul. You must accept suffering as a growing experience, and seeing her pain, there are times it is hard on those by him or her. I am not so cruel, yet believe that her soul has much light and will leave... Truly believe this light is radiating from her only because of your prayer; only because you have touched.*"

"But this woman has been a good mother, a good wife, and has led a good life," I countered. "How can you say the light radiates from her only because I touched her?"

"Not only. Much of her light is her own. Yours has just aided her and elevated her. Has made the brightness far-reaching. Can you trust and accept what you cannot see? Can you accept that ill fortune and suffering must be inflicted? I cannot change the mechanisms, for there is a purpose.

"There will be a time when she will realize how much you have touched her, and how much you have truly comforted her. If you were to do nothing else in your life; if you were to never have written your book; if you never advance, and never go on to touch all those souls, yet this one insight were to take place, accept that -- know that -- your one tiny deed, one act, will shine and shine throughout eternity.

"I should not have taxed her (Rosalyn) this time. My blessings are within you. I bestow them upon (you). I can kiss the top of your head, but know that I am carried within you; that a part of that light will shine to any who see you. You know that it is necessary to take this away.

"I should have made you start earlier. Should have put an obstacle (presumably to prevent us from getting together with the others tonight). *I would have wished to have had some prepare the two of you very specially early, and come before Me rested, and when energy is strong."*

I asked why He didn't come through me, since I felt strong.

"I know you do. You have much energy within you. Much energy. You do not reach inside and pull it up. The way you wish to take the pain away from your aunt; I know how eager you are to take the pain away the same way. I do not go directly throughout you. Accept there must be a sharing, and she has a gift that was placed within her....

"You will see. You must lead. You do receive. Do not concern yourself, for you do not, you truly receive from Me. You will see many things unfurl before you. You will understand why it is appropriate this way. I... have my... love within you. When you act, you are acting in My aim. You will feel what is going to be instilled within you. You will just perform. You will just say. You will not be channeled. It will be you speaking My words (and indeed, that's exactly the way any messages I have ever gotten have come through). *I will not interfere. I have done it to some extent. I am bestowing My blessings upon...please, the benevolence this night. Have patience, and faith in Me..."*

Rosalyn came out of it amazed. "Oh, Howard, there's such brightness. Like it's going up. It'd draped around you. I almost can't see through it. The light is inside you. There's so much brightness inside you."

September 19, 1987
At my apartment with Rosalyn.

She went off quickly. We received a message, allegedly from the powerful angel Raziel, who told us that he was nearby, inspiring and protecting us, and that I should not rush through the final stages of putting Enoch and the Book of Coincidences together.

"*This book will be sealed*," he said. "*You must use it as a foundation for what you know you are here for.*" He explained that there were others waiting to come through who felt he was "*monopolizing*" us. He faded, and for many moments there was silence. Then:

"*I send you greetings. I, too, are very pleased that you are writing a book. You were with me many occasions with my writing.*" I knew instantly that this had to be PA.

"*I know who you are now. The only one who can see Matthew is Aliasha. She does not see the present person. I've told you I've missed many of our talks. Sometimes I have lectured you, but it has, even if you do not understand how, still remained through all your lifetimes.*

"*You are performing a deed that I still feel pride in seeing grow to fruition. The many talks, many discussions have been carried through the ages. I feel the tension of the hours. However, if you can picture the daylight, the beautiful country I picture, I can stand in that age. Like a spring day, the sun was bright and I had your love with me. No one would interrupt us. There were many chores you performed for me I knew there were times you wished to be with her. There were many times you had things to scurry to. But you did it, somehow. You never quite frowned. At least, not in front of me.*

"*She would sometimes go out of her way to see that I had eaten. How I loved you both so much. I should not make you feel melancholy, or add to any burdens that lay heavy upon you this day. Presently you are both still young, though I know you would never let her presently think that* (pretty cute -- I did, in fact, continually rib Rosalyn about her age). *But there is much that can be accomplished, and so much that does lie before you. I appreciate that I still am permitted to contact you. It is easier to remain in the past, to put my mind at ease. But that will not assist you now.*"

As we spoke I could tell that PA was fading. Rosalyn's tone of voice altered slightly, and I soon found that Aliasha had replaced him.

"Matthew. I am finding something difficult. I know somehow, I know, I remember, speaking with you (she must have meant back on August 29). I remember that you do not look as Matthew. I do not understand how this was possible. I'm sorry. I still feel as if permissible to call you Matthew. I sense that being, and yet I am being filled with something, and it's as if I'm on one side feeling, I suppose, (a) message of some kind, ands yet I'm giving it to you on a different side. There's a high hope you do not think that I am delirious, but I... Matthew, it's strange. I'm not certain if I am in a dream, and I have seen you, but this time I can sense he's (Philo's) here. He's speaking. Somehow he's speaking. Matthew -- please do not let me be lost. I don't understand...

"I think... said to have (his) quill and... though is not quite the same now. Why do you always seem to be recording something? I can see him... but he's not where you are... I think now, like crossing over something... He's, Matthew, he's here. He's standing with us. Can you see him as I do?"

"No, I can't."

"Then we are not in the same place. I am very confused..."

I asked whether Aliasha was in contact with any of those who were around Jesus. "I did not have much more contact with any of them after we separated. I do not see Mary very often."

I next asked her about Mary and the supposed virgin birth. "Did anyone ever speak of it to you?"

"Yes. I remember women talking. They said something that Joseph is not his father. Then, when we heard him speak, he said he was 'of his father.' We were uncertain of our thoughts."

"Did Mary say anything about it?"

"She said he was of the radiance. She could not ever speak ill of Joseph. She loved him. I think they lived as husband and wife. And Jesus showed him respect. Did not state (he was his) father. Some said what you know, he was from God. Oh, Matthew," she continued, shaking her head, "we used to talk so much, and many times we felt strongly in what he said. What we heard him speak of other times we would feel so strong of our own convictions. I felt a love from him. I was in his presence, and

I'd heard Mary speak of him."

"Did you know Joseph?"

"No."

"Then, he left Mary?"

"I don't know. I know many times she was not with anyone. She was by herself and wished for company, as you say. She had much grief. She was his mother. One stayed with her after. John. He, I think, told him to feel that she was his mother also. I don't know many of those people.

"You know how I cried. We spoke one afternoon, and things were so difficult that time. No matter what someone does, they should not be condemned. So many stories were told after his death; makes you wonder what was true."

I asked her what Philo thought of the virgin birth story. "You spoke to him as much as I! I think... the two of you kind of looked at me like I was so innocent. You did not believe such a thing... Difficult to accept, but I think -- I do not think Mary would tell untruth."

"Did Mary actually say it was a virgin birth?"

"She never said, really. She... One day, you and he really pestered me. You tried persuading me completely that it was made up. I do not think she would... There always seemed to be somebody (saying), 'God told me this, I am a prophet.' There was so much of that.

And I think sometimes we used to laugh about the different men that would pass through, and they'd always have some kind of messages, and we kind of wondered when the next one would come up.

"But I think, with what I'm beginning to sense last time and now, that that life was truly a time for many to have God's words. Maybe we just couldn't see it. There was only that one that truly made us question. I don't know if you can relate to that time. Do you think you ever would have completely turned away? I don't think you ever could have. I know you listened to me a great deal, what I would talk of my feelings and being in a quandary. I don't think as much as... I felt for the words, and Mary. I do not think you could have ever rejected everything that was so much part of us."

I asked Aliasha if she knew Philo's brother, Bressen (he had told us months before that he had tried to win her after Matthew left, but that Philo prevented it because his desire for her wasn't of a spiritual nature). Rosalyn became visibly coy, and she sounded like a child trying to worm out of an embarrassing situation without outright lying.

"Did *I* know him? He, wait... wait...." she tittered. "He lived in another place, Matthew. Not the same town. He...... I think maybe we should talk about something else."

September 24, 1987
Rosh Hashana, the Jewish New Year -- sitting alone in my apartment.

I was wondering whether my conclusions about Jesus, Christianity, and Judaism -- which I had just started recording in Enoch and the Book of Coincidences -- were right. They seemed correct, based on everything we'd gotten. But still, I was dealing with such a monumental statement here. What if I was misinterpreting something? Was I sure I'd considered everything? I absentmindedly picked up a pen to see if anything happened. It did, with a rush.

You are right! You are right! You are correct. He is as you say. He was a son, as are all My children. He was not a God, nor shall they pray to him any longer. He was and always will be a proud standard bearer. He is a shining light in the firmament, but he is not the source of light. You have recognized this, now they must, too.

They have long forgotten what their forebears knew well. There is but one God, and His name is One. Resounding. There are none to compare. Hashem is the light of eternity. The lights of the poles shine from Me, and the oceans crest and ebb because of Me. Let no one declare that he is afraid to hear these truths. Let no one be recalcitrant. I alone may judge. I alone may sit upon the throne and pass judgement on man.

Off in the distance I saw young men in robes, and seemed to feel that they would be prophets in the future.

For I will make them (these new prophets) *say something that will shock the world: I am He from whom the Holocaust sprang. I am the generator of all things. Those things that are necessary I have made to happen. The scheme is far too vast for mortal eyes to see in its entirety. Trust must accompany faith. Trust in faith, as your forefathers declared their faith in Me when I delivered them from the bonds of slavery. Even then they were stubborn, but at least they acknowledged My existence, if only to disdain it.*

This generation is rampant, fearing nothing and caring about their stomachs, not their souls. The lipstick (representing material comforts and luxury) *will be wiped from their faces, slowly. It will be smeared and painted on blood. They must listen and heed Me through My servant, Howard. He is to be My regent. He will deliver My words unto the masses, that they may quake in fear and huddle together and await my judgment.*

Follow the decrees he has passed on to you. They are My words as faithfully written down by a trustworthy scribe. Let no man declare him to be a false prophet, for My voice and My anger will be raised against them, and they will know My wrath.

They will feel hurt, and they will come to know the truth. He is My voice at this time. By his words you shall heed. Pay attention to them. Scrutinize them. Learn them as law. They are the revealed word. Punishment awaits those who mock them. Draw nigh to me, lest thou be consumed by the fire that will range abroad, across the land. Furnace heat......

There was no more.

September 29, 1987

Rosalyn, writing alone at home.

My daughter, concentrate. Do not lose hope. You are on a tip (we'd heard that expression before; it referred to the tip of an angel's wing; in other words, we were being guided).

There is a great deal within you that must be given out to others. You will find some seeking you. Be very discreet in your circle. Trust in the one you had confidence in (Jesus). *He can guide you as you were guiding him* (me). *Remember, you fuse as one. Discouragement should be overcome. Each one needs to instill and enlighten the other. Sit and meditate again each day and my messages will become clearer to you. Try each night to sense My essence inside you. You remain hesitant and frightened. You still need his serene influence and direction surrounding you.*

Do not relent. I am not willing to have what has been nurtured dissipate. The two of you are recognizing the union which has been thwarted in past. His words are golden. Encourage him, as you know he is specially chosen, and your connection to enhance the other has been preordained. His heat will heal the righteous and shall also scald the wicked.

With that, Rosalyn said, she heard an enormously loud noise, "like thunder cracking," and awoke "jolted and disoriented. I felt lost."

October 1, 1987

On a business trip to Washington, D.C.

I found some white candles in my hotel room, so when I got all settled in I lit one and prayed. Then I wrote.

Clouds purify, wet the land. Dew dries upon the Earth. Holy rain kisses the Earth. The roses blush and the air is melodious. Life finds its way out of shelter and into the air. No one dares mock you. You are faithful. Your words are true, even if you yourself doubt them sometimes. Have heart.

October 4, 1987

On the phone with Rosalyn.

After a few minutes she said she could see the word *Jesus* spelled out in front of her. There was a long silence, then:

"I will always be with you. Never doubt that I have comforted you. Listen to his words. Some truths. Not all has been revealed yet. You will not lose me. It is important that the two most meaningful ones connect (meaning, I assume, the "two most meaningful" religions, Judaism and Christianity*). The beliefs shall interlock. They may not become one, but shall come to realize they must compromise. It is very minutely begun in a social way."*

Rosalyn's demeanor changed subtly. Moments passed, and I could tell someone else was coming through.

"My daughter, you are relating to him as My son. You must also begin to think honestly and sincerely about the words written before you (in Enoch and the Book of Coincidences).

"H is attempting to combine knowledge which has been, in some ways, deceptively hidden. He will need your support and spiritual advice. Do not rift (sic) *from one another. There is a great deed which will still be felt. Do not let yourself part from him now. Think, think honestly. Give unto him when he requests your guidance. You will not be abandoned. Your beliefs are strong, and yet you have been open enough to look at what is being unfolded before you. H is trying to show you.*

"H: Continue your research. Continue to be close to her. She will need you more, and you are the only one who will finally reach her. Be aware of her concerns and realize there is a great deal to what she believes. You will receive more insights also.

The two of you bring an energy unprecedented when you are united."

October 11, 1987

The gang at Teresa's.

Our hostess began doing the board.

HI. I AM MICHAEL. ANGEL. GIVE ME YOUR BLESSINGS...
MATTHEW IS HERE.

This was baffling. I couldn't recall Michael, the archangel, ever coming through Teresa before. Nor could I recall her getting Matthew, either. Later on, Teresa was still on the board when she slipped into a trance, and started speaking rather than reading the messages.

"David is near," she said. I looked at Rosalyn. Neither of us had ever said a single word to any of the others about David or anything connected with all the messiah talk. "H comes with him. Tell David to go to the water."

"Are you referring to me as David?" I asked.

"Sometimes," Teresa continued. "You must be cleansed to be more of me."

"Tell me more about David," I said.

"Is near woman, Ruth (Ruth was King David's grandmother, but I doubt very strongly that Teresa knew this). Why, I don't understand. David is talking. Can't understand what he's saying. He is with many from pyramids with him. Stone floor. Long hall. Marble steps. Stand on them to talk. I am David..."

I asked what the connection was between David and Joseph.

"Same spirit; like one," Teresa murmured. "Same stone from the walk. You must know the feeling from both. Joseph carried you once."

"I don't understand that."

"He sent for you many times."

"Do you mean Joseph or the Son of Joseph?"

"Joseph. Too much for you now."

"You mean Old Testament Joseph?"

"Yes."

I asked what the connection was between Joseph and Jesus.

"Not yet to connect. Not yet for the path you must accept now. What comes must come." With that, Teresa pulled her hands off the board and slowly reawakened, feeling distinctly puzzled about what she'd gotten.

But the impact had registered with me. I know that Teresa knew nothing about David, or my alleged connection to him, or about Joseph, and his alleged connection to Jesus. Those things had only come through when Rosalyn and I were alone.

But now Teresa was apparently getting it. That was important. It meant that Rosalyn was no longer the sole source of all this stuff; I had independent confirmation that this wasn't all a product of Rosalyn's imagination. I now had it from two sources. As a reporter, it pleased me no end. And as someone who was doubting his sanity more than ever, well... it was nice.

Just before midnight Rosalyn took the board.

PREPARE FOR THE ARRIVAL. YOU WILL ACCEPT IT.... INNER SELVES KNOW TRUTH... BRING LIGHT TO THE WORLD... ALWAYS KEEP BOND. WAIT FOR ANSWERS. U ARE SIMPLY PASTING PIECES TOGETHER. ALL WILL FIT INTO ONE.

JOSHUA IS AROUND. CIRCLE OF PROTECTION ALWAYS... I HAVE COME TO THIS WELL MANY TIMES. I GREET U, THOUGH STRANGERS, WITH KINDNESS. YOUR EYES SHOW SOMETHING SPECIAL. I SHALL SEE U ONE DAY HENCE MANY YEARS. WHEN I LOOK IN YOUR EYES, THEN I SHALL REMEMBER WHAT I SAW LIFETIMES PREVIOUS. I WILL OFFER MY LOVE TO U. I CAN SEE THE KINDNESS IN YOUR EYES. U ARE TO BE CHOSEN. U ARE HE THEY AWAIT. I AM NOT A POOR GIRL...

From what we'd gotten in the past about Miriam and our meeting at the well, I have to assume this was her speaking. Rosalyn started to feel uncomfortable, and started to trance.

"Children of Israel shall not reject. They must adhere to what has been told to them. If they reject, many ills shall befall them. Too many signs have been laid in front. They are sent the one, and do not see it. If they refute the book, they shall feel the wrath once more. All has been placed within you. All is laden inside.

"Wars and strife brought on by man. They lead to self-annihilation. One unity shall bring calm to troubled masses. It is not easy. Continue your prayers. They strengthen inside and out; for except for their assistance, you will stand alone.

"One great test before you. You shall have to proceed. No retreat now. Your life will become one with... You are the one in the light... stem from you. This is the ultimate pinnacle. Utilize wisely, and give over gently and generously..."

October 14, 1987

The four of us at Rosalyn's house. She saw a man white a long white beard.

"I have led you through the wilderness. You must lead... have been waiting for one to resume. Your battles will be fought with words..."

October 16, 1987

At my apartment with Rosalyn. She asked for a pen and paper.

May I enter your dwelling? I am a traveler from a great distance. I bring only peace and greetings. There is much warmth here, and welcome for the weary. I am a representative of something, as you sense. The hands felt touching your hair (Rosalyn's, and yes, she had felt something like that) *were those of many you have reached with your love and goodness. I am to open the doorway, for your children cling to my robes. They can sense the love.*

Rosalyn began to speak.

"*Your fingers must do my work. Each one holds different meaning. Thumb holds the words to... you hold the key to unlock many. Do you not share words? Do you not offer a prayer together? Does not every new... leader have his crest... and must befit you to also have insignia...*

"*Yes, I can be proud. Follow your destiny. A true... son of David will never waiver. You are the true... I have been placed in your path...*

"*You are interlocking pieces, and do not allow forces that know how close you are to detach you, for they do not want this link. They do not want the strength one gives the other.*"

Later that night, Rosalyn felt once more that she had to write. Soon she began to speak.

"*Do you believe what has been written? Do you believe this is that which is penned by you is that which is truth?.... There shall be resistance. There shall be family versus family. There will be much dissension.*"

"As a result of my book?" I asked.

"*That is one ultimate. It will begin... then it shall catapult. It will be widespread. Secretly, you will learn. Be aware of the impact for time. It will seem as if not accepted.*

"*They will come together... You will be sought by those who believe. You will be scorned and ridiculed by those who disbelieve, and those who are frightened to accept. You will need much strength. You need to follow your visions. You need to pull all together.*"

"*Howard,*" she said, "*there's some sort of cloud, and it's, like, it's traveling. Like worldwide illness; like people are... there's an epidemic, or dying...*

"*Beware of one who will attempt to bring... You will face against him. He..... they are trying all this* time. They will have to....no. No. There is too much light around him (meaning me). *He cannot reach you this time... There are angels who will not relent. They are strong. They are a circle of light and protection. They are here because you are he who must lead the righteous. You shall also feel the right to exude wrath...*

"*You will see what lies before you. You have glimpsed some of what is there. You know that what you write and what you envision and what is placed within the book stems from us. Our fire is within you. It is burning to go forth. Is unquenchable need for knowledge. You will always ask. I cannot admonish your inquisitiveness. It is part of the makeup of the man that...*

"*You will encounter many who will start to question after they read what has been brought together. They will not have the inner turmoil that she who is behind you* (does). *They will encounter some. You as a king and as a.... Speak. You are permitted.*"

I asked a question that had been troubling me for some time. "What," I wanted to know, "is there in the New Testament that is valid, that's true?'

"You would need hours. You have scholars who are trained to... They will point. There is confusion, but it is necessary to have such a belief... Formulate. You will see the proper phases. Where do you feel most uneasy? Do you... you cannot... you cannot doubt your own words. Must not happen."

I asked whether Christians could be considered idolaters for bowing in front of the cross.

"If they commit this, all religions are committing this. They are believers in what they are doing. Much has been distorted. What should have been belief became distorted. There was a reason for religion to stem, but man caused symbols. Man created crosses. Man created the statues."

I distinctly didn't like the statement that all religions were committing idolatry. What about Judaism, whose main tenet is to fight idolatry?

"All are before the symbols, as you feel about Christians. Jews, your own, do not. There are many symbols, down to even primitive tribes. Their idols are worshiped, but they truly believe in what lies behind. Shall they all be condemned?"

"Shall they all be condemned?" I said. "What about the second commandment -- 'Thou shalt not bow down before graven images?"

"Second commandment for Jews. They (Christians) *are not the Chosen. They are not within His light. They are following belief of ancestors. They are, in their hearts, true believers. They have not seen, experienced, the true light. You carry that."*

"In other words," I said, trying to understand what I was being told and still not sure of who I was speaking to, "it's okay for anyone who's not Jewish to bow down before an idol?"

"Does not your commandment, as you state, command that theirs is not as strong? They are relying upon some form to place before them. They, some, need the grasp of solid form, something to focus upon. Do you understand me?"

"In other words you're saying that only the Jews are able to grasp the concept of an invisible God, while the others need something palpable to look at?"

"True."

I asked another question I'd been wondering about. "Why are there Christians at all? Why was that religion created?"

"There was much conflict which would... mankind was.... experienced strife. We.... they were destined to suffer."

"You mean the Jews?"

"Yes."

"Why?"

"They were highest expectation. They are special, and cannot tolerate. There is one.... not 20. They, as the Chosen, exhibit responsibility. Do you follow me?"

"You mean, because they had to adhere to a stricter code of law, and they haven't?"

"Of course. They first were mine (Mine?). *They would have had the luxury of splendor, of fruitfulness. No struggle."*

"Haven't the Jews suffered because it was a way of purifying them?"

"They will always become closer, for they are attempting what you state."

"Did Jesus know that his coming would result in persecution and suffering of his own people?"

"Yes."

"Why was he selected?"

"Why were you selected?"

"................ I don't know," I said honestly.

"There is much you must overcome. There is much inner strife. There are impurities. There are many consequences of what surrounds you. They will be overcome. Confidence is placed inside you."

"Will I have to overcome them by suffering?"

"Not entirely. You have altered many things. You will continue to...."

"Did Jesus claim to be the messiah?"

"Was not stated. Was not uttered, but specific moment.... You will find difficulty in answering for........."

"What about what we call The Theory? That, if Rosalyn and I had hooked up back then and not been separated, the Apocalypse and the Salvation would have happened 2,000 years ago?"

"How will that affect you?" (Very interesting. Once again, a thread that has run through all of our sessions: a very definite concern on the part of the various speakers for our emotional well-being, of not wanting to give us more than we could cope with.) *"Why do.... I hesitate to respond, but I state that I may not answer all questions. After the response I told you, yes."*

"Does that mean that yes, The Theory is correct?"

"Yes."

"Well, why was evil, or the force of darkness, allowed to prevent us from hooking up?"

"What force tried to interfere when you and she were first banded? You recognized it (Fredericke, who though he was no longer threatening Rosalyn had come to embody the dark side, for want of a better term, or the forces of evil). *I have placed evil within all creation, and to My dismay there were many instances where you turned from Me. You, as My creation, mankind, was given free will. You were told*

many have waited for this connection. You are to... Believe what has been said to you."

"But the 'forces of darkness' exist, don't they?"

"Yes."

"Is the Jewish belief correct, that the devil is your faithful servant?"

"How do you read that statement? Why is that view?"

I said I didn't understand the question.

"How do you believe that statement is meant? What is your theory?"

I answered that, since God controls absolutely everything that happens, that whatever evil the devil did, it was God doing it. Or at least, it was God who was not preventing it.

"As man has free will for good, the evil has free will. That is how it existed. I do not place My hand down to prevent what foolishness transpires. Creation was for............. I do not condone evil. It is begun and it coexists. You may have to discontinue soon (Rosalyn was shivering, and occasionally wrenching herself to one side or the other. She was clearly uncomfortable). *I will not abandon the session. Think."*

I went on the assumption that this was, indeed, somehow... God.

"You do have an active hand in the world, in that you maintain its existence at every second. Why don't you prevent evil?"

"That is of your own volition. I do not step in for the good as well. It is not that I could ever condone. You have been placed with free will, and it is because of this there is still suffering. Foolishness. Such ignorance."

"God created us," I continued. "How could he expect anything else?"

"If one can be so holy and one can be so good, I did not influence that one as I did not influence the evil. You were created and given free will. It has caused much annihilation. If I prevent, then all will cease to exist."

"Why?"

"For if I shall interfere, then is no purpose."

"Well, what about back in Egypt, when you took my people out of bondage with a 'strong hand' (by punishing Egypt with plagues and ultimately parting the Red Sea). That was sure interference."

"That is My people. That was your beginnings. Did not examples of God need to be shown? They must have seen God for your history to recall ages of their.... happenings."

"Why was the Holocaust necessary?"

"Holocaust was atrocious. It was evil personified. It showed throughout ensuing years... Destruction...... for the suffering people....... The personification of evil is manifested strongest that time."

"And what about your Chosen People?" I said with more than a hint of irony in my voice. What was I trying to do, make God feel guilty? Yes.

"And all the suffering and all the people have to show how they still have not banded to God. What stronger example..... Belief suffered. Their faith is still strongest."

"Does absolutely everything that happens have a purpose?"

"Not any meaningful one."

"How many years ago was the world created?"

"Why do you always question? Man will always fight his own theory. He argues among selves. Why is it necessary to think how long (ago) the world was created? I exist always and always, and creation is not.........."

With a violent lurch, Rosalyn started to come out of her trance. She called out my name, and I took hold of her hand and tried to calm her. She awoke telling me about a "huge, huge ball of flame" that was fading away.

At the end, the same thought struck me that had occurred to me many times before. How could all this, these messages, be nothing more than Rosalyn's subconscious mind? She -- and don't get mad at me for saying this, Rosalyn -- just isn't smart enough to come up with answers to all my questions, many of which were rather deep, wise, and thought-provoking – and on the spur of the moment. Neither was I. Neither of us possessed the breadth of knowledge needed to give many of the responses we'd gotten. It simply could not be her. Then what was the explanation?

Had I really just argued with God?

October 20, 1987

All of us at Teresa's, who once again started things off on the board.

THE BIND IS STRONG. THE KNOT SHALL NOT BE UNLOOSED.... KEEP CERTAIN SESSIONS PRIVATE... U KNOW WHAT CIRCUMSTANCES ARE TO REMAIN SILENT. THIS SESSION WILL NOW BEGIN.

Rosalyn and I gaped at each other. It was happening again; Teresa was getting things that were familiar to the two of us, but which she couldn't possibly know. How could she have known that the two of us, when alone, received the same warnings against speaking of the messiah business? Answer: she couldn't have known.

October 21, 1987

At my place with Rosalyn.

PA (Philo of Alexandria) came through, first on the board, then through Rosalyn. I asked some questions about the nature of prayers, and which ones get answered.

"Do not question Him. His ways are not for us to change. I am not so answerable. I am not one who has been permitted so intimate an answer. I will tell you, my son, that you are acting as you see correct.

But do not question, although circumstances are difficult for you to see."

I asked about "The Theory." What would have happened if Matthew and Aliasha had hooked up as they were supposed to so long ago?

"This would have been the light I await for my eyes. I was always grateful for the love I shared between you. I know of terrible suffering and bitter strife. So much could have been negated. You have come too close. I shall never endure separation again. The two must seal. Do not give in to what seems to be splitting around you. He (Fredericke, once again personifying those who were the enemies of God), *too, can gain. He works different method this time around. Cannot. And do not doubt that you are the reason he has not taken her. You are a light around her. You are like an electrified fence, and he can feel you. You shan't be prevented again. You can't allow this."*

I asked next how history would have been altered if Matthew and Aliasha had not been separated.

"There would have been so much peace. There (would) *have been closeness, humanity. There should have been beautiful offspring. No one could deny the love that grew. So many lives would not have been lost, for the purity in your souls when united, would have been blinding to the evil."*

"Why did all this happen during the time of Jesus?"

"There..... the new faith that.... he brought love and peace. You sensed what was exuded from him. You absorbed some of that light. Your connections are of complete circle, which is different. Your purity to one another was needed."

I asked whether there was any prophecy concerning two young people who would affect all of history by being separated from each other.

"I do not recall any. I know it was felt in my heart. I knew what was sensed from. I do not know why they did not prevent the separation, as I cannot explain why the situation continues with your friend. I know I will always try to be near you, and to stand by you when you need it, if I am permitted to do so."

Next, I asked where Elijah was in all this. Jewish tradition held that he was supposed to precede the messiah. If I'm being told I am the messiah, I reasoned, where's Elijah?

"You truly are pressuring me. I wish I could give you so many answers. Some I am not certain of. I will tell you he is almost the final step. Trust in that."

I asked PA whether the legend that Enoch and Elijah were actually one and the same person was true.

"I cannot answer you. I cannot. I tell you how proud I am of you. I truly hope that some of your answers will be given very shortly. I will be leaving soon."

"Is there any validity to those stories about statues bleeding and holes suddenly appearing in people's palms?"

"Palms are true."

"And the statues?"

"A few."

"But don't those things violate the laws of nature?"

"Yes, but it is part of His strong connection to their extreme devotion. You have no idea of what the mind can accomplish."

"You mean these things are all created by the mind?"

"No. I have said some of devotion is all that can ever be described. They are enduring physical pain. I knew Matthew, when you sat so many hours, you had a strong mind and curiosity then. It will tax me now, for you have very valid statements. My son, I only hope I will be allowed to give you some answers. I do not know....."

PA faded momentarily, but soon returned. The time had come to ask the big question.

"Am I the Messiah, Son of David?"

"You ask this answer of me? As a messenger, it is not for me to respond. I say this: Many holy ones have come to you. Many puzzles you unraveled. Even my communication to you is of great significance. I would be honored to give an answer. It is not I that may. You know how close all the pieces are coming. You will feel great exuberance. I must depart."

And he did.

October 24, 1987

At Rosalyn's.

After being told by a spirit guide that Joshua's "honor guard" was around us to protect us, Rosalyn sensed the angel Michael.

"Yes, R. You are learning to sense me more easily. H: unknown reason you did not sense what she felt was coming. It should have reached you. It is one of those snags that were attempting to break down the link (between Rosalyn and myself). *The two are not aware of how much closer you are, but some outside forces are. It will be incumbent upon you to close selves. You may need to draw upon each other for answers. This is to enforce around you while some are trying to get into your bond.*

"There, as we have told you, are those who know your power. If you hold to each other, you will gain the strength and insight in the other to receive what message or vision is to be given you... Remember, you need each other's strength and support because there is... as a thrust or a surge that must be absorbed and sensed within each of you which will place you on a high plateau... I know he (Fredericke) *has been appraised of your words. I know it will be complete soon. You have great gift. You are chosen to have the words*

sound as necessary for proper people to intake. It is as a hypnotic effect."

What follows, I can only interpret as some sort of... *fight.*

"They can't take their words. They can't. You can't, can't have his words. You... he will also protect me and light will be around him. No. This much has been accomplished. I will not allow you to stop him. They will encircle.

"No. No! No! He is a part of me. Now at this time, I do believe in his words. You will not prevent him. You.... light will be too strong for you. The light surrounding him. The light is around her, and he is the one you fear. But you will never, you can never penetrate him.

"Outside, he is circled by angels and soldiers. I (am) only an instrument to help speak and be a part of him. But you will never break the bond. You will never cause it again. Go away! You... I am not going to be (weak? tricked?). *I am not.... there are too many here to help. Don't you ever, EVER touch him! Don't you try to take those words. They are golden. What...."*

Rosalyn jerked from side to side, shaking her head as if to say, 'No, no, no...' I placed my hands on top of her head and, as had happened in the past, within minutes she calmed down.

"There was somebody ashen, just all white, almost like he had powder all over his face," she said when she regrouped. "And he wanted you. But, like, he was... like it was your words he wanted to pull away. Like he didn't want any of your words to be heard.

"You were there," she continued. "Michael was here, but it was between him and I. There were angels, like soldiers, and you were like locked; part of me. You were special, and you were being prevented from seeing it. Yet part of me was you, and it was like what happened to you happened to me. He (the ashen one) was strong. He wasn't nice. He had some kind of cape, like the high-collared type. It just exuded something. It was like protection for him."

And just before she went limp, she added, she saw the name *Fredericke* in front of her.

October 31, 1987

At Rosalyn's. Michele and Teresa had just left.

BOOK IS UNIQUE. BOOK IS MASTERPIECE. HOLD WITH RESPECT. PETER WALKED WITH U ONCE. TOLD U SOME DAY U WOULD KNOW YOUR DESTINY... SAID TWO LIFETIMES WOULD BECOME ONE. TWO WOULD MEET...

Just then Rosalyn said she was seeing a man dressed in a suit and glasses, holding a briefcase right in front of her. He was blocking the message, she said. I told her to think of the gold Book of Raziel, and of Joshua's armies protecting us. He disappeared.

HOWARD: U ARE MICHAEL. U ARE TO SAVE MANY. U ARE THE ONE COMBINATION OF MANY. U KNOW HOW DESPERATION

HAS BEEN PLACED IN U, AND FROM WHOSE GUIDANCE IT IS
COME.

"Whatever I do is done because I believe it's what God wants," I
said.

THAT IS THE ONLY ONE U PAY HOMAGE TO.

Near the end of our session Rosalyn saw "a wreath around your
head; something's that's destined for you."

November 6, 1987

Rosalyn started to drift off on my couch.

*"When some look upon you, you appear to be two innocent
children. I have seen men who have waited years and years and never
received signs you have seen, you have sensed. You have the power
inside you. You are not ready. You do not understand. You do feel
many vibrations. You intercede powerfully. You anticipate her need,
then....... You would be inapproachable. You shall stand apart. You will
feel vibration there."*

I asked what the speaker meant by saying that I would be
inapproachable.

*"Many should not reach you directly. There will be a circle around
you at all times. There will be those trusting and those who are loyal
who will advise you, have comprehending mind. You have
intuitiveness. You truly are the core of her relating. Never doubt there is
a special gift endowed inside her, but it is opened with your key, and it
will walk with you. She is also placed to be there for you. That is her
purpose.*

*"You will receive a full..... They will consist of people from where
you least expect. They will seek you and you will respond. You will not
realize where it's coming from. There's a pen always at your side. Your
words flow like a stream of water. They perfectly show what is meant to
be revealed. Do you believe anyone could have concluded and joined
together the data you compiled?"*

"Yes," I said, "some people."

*"No. They would not concern themselves and they do not reach
deep within, which is where yours has truly been instilled. I am only a
speaker. I see who stands before me. I see one who will lead.*

*"I see two moons. I see people who have lost all faith. I see you...
stands out, for you reinforce that. You save their souls, you who seem
very inadequate. You are the one they will call. Do not allow.... You will
place your hand upon them and what you pray to surround them will.
You will bring them up from the bottom of all. The least likely shall rise
above. There are words that need to be spoken. There is much to be
written, you are to write, and it is in your writing that certain things will
be understood. The light shoots through you."*

Rosalyn stopped talking and started blindly feeling around for the
pad. I gave it to her with a pen. In an eerie scrawl, she wrote:

You and she bring...... must feel what it is you are preaching to them. At times you will not realize you are preaching, but your guidance shall be their only hope -- you may not sense what is reaching... for a long period, but then others will seek you. Your wisdom and insight.....

"*I see you as you are,*" Rosalyn said, only half awake. "*I see somebody coming to you for counsel, advice, and you won't realize this is part of what you're supposed to do. You won't realize how grateful. One leads to the other, and all of a sudden there's this group, a crowd, whatever. Something will happen to make many people upset. It will be to you they'll end up coming. You are the one who can pull them together. You are the one to do something for them.*"

At 4:49 am, Rosalyn was lying asleep on my bed, and I went to the bathroom. When I came back Rosalyn was grasping the pillow and sobbing hysterically. Hysterically! It took several minutes for me to quiet her down. When she finally did get calm she drifted off once more. She started murmuring something about someone being angry at the both of us.

"Why?" I asked.

"*You did not open* (the session with a prayer as we were told in the past that we must), *and both should have sealed. I have said you are to seal yourselves. Too much..... You must put your lights and protection around you before he* (Fredericke?) *shall try to reach her. He knows you are too strong. Your seal of one another must be done. You are close to the heavens. Cannot.... there are much elevated paths to his light.*

"*You are not being faulted for leaving her. You and she did not lose the protection that surrounds you. The individual light that you should envision encircling you was missing. She was too powerful all week, but you need to realize there is much more power each week. You that they see. They know.*"

I pointed out that Joshua's armies were supposed to be protecting us. And what about the psalm that reads, 'The God of Israel neither slumbers nor sleeps.' So how, I demanded, did any evil force get through to us?

"*Because she allowed an opening this.... You must.... it is not.....*"

Rosalyn said she saw the letters E-N-0-C-H "lit up" in front of her. I took the offensive.

"This is a direct result of you guys keeping me in the dark and not letting me experience any of it firsthand," I bellowed. "If I had, I could help combat it. I blame YOU! And there you have it!"

"*You are justified. What has she felt..... even though questioning most....*"

After a few minutes Rosalyn said she felt she was "supposed to go. I don't know where, but this will make room for someone to come in. I'm being scolded...."

The message began to filter through.

"She must be serious. She must do some (religious) *ritual every day. She must realize that the two of you are sealing because of this book, because of the words, it is not a joke. There are many angles being pulled at her. Many everyday occurrences are not ordinary. There is... outside. I do not wish for an opening to yet occur. Michael. You create difficulty."*

"Who, me?" I asked.

"Not you. She is detaching. Cannot permit this to occur."

This was true. Rosalyn had been telling me for a long while that she was finding it increasingly hard to pray, especially to go to church. Perhaps there was no connection, but in recent weeks the messages had been coming through more weakly than ever. She clutched at her twitching arm.

"The arm has been stretched across because you have not held fast to this link. It is necessary tonight to return to the apprehension she once felt. You must get through to her. I am coming in, my son, to try to clear her up. I do not like so many people pulling at her." I asked who this was speaking now.

"Do you not know me? I am PA. I am trying to clear her. Hopefully, then, you would receive clear messages."

Moments later, he was gone, Rosalyn was asleep and I was -- as usual -- left feeling frustrated. However, something important had become clear. The way she'd gone off the deep end when I left the room for a few fleeting moments. Something, as we had suspected, was definitely after us. Fredericke's minions, apparently. And it could only really get at Rosalyn when the two of us were separated.

And I was scheduled to leave for France on business in a week .

November 9, 1987

Rosalyn wasn't the only one going through emotional turmoil.

I was miserable. Here I was taking part in this strange phenomenon and being told on a regular basis that I was the messiah. *Could I seriously believe that I was the messiah?* Only a madman would -- right? And if it was, somehow, true? Then I was sitting on the biggest secret in the history of the world. People were getting famous on TV talk shows with stories of supernatural phenomena nowhere near as important as this. Shouldn't I be doing something? Saving people? Leading armies? Ending tyranny somewhere in the world? Performing miracles? Chatting with Oprah or Phil? I joked with Rosalyn that my opening act as the redeemer would be to levitate the World Trade Center (both towers).

I'd been nearly obsessing about this for weeks. Then I cracked open a volume by the revered Rabbi Moshe ben Nachman (better known as the Ramban) in which he speaks of the messiah. It said that the tribulations that the messiah would undergo when he arrived on Earth would not be physical.

"(They are) only the grief which he experiences because his coming is very greatly delayed. He sees his people in exile (living outside Israel) and there is nought in the power of his hand."

Sounded strangely like the emotional upset I was going through now. Was this another of our coincidences? Was it conceivable that the wise old sage had somehow peaked into the soul of the messiah centuries ago...... and seen *me?*

November 12, 1987

Flipping through the channels on TV as I talked with my mother on the phone. I got to the credits for "Napoleon and Josephine" just in time to see the name Fredericke.

And I was leaving for France in two days.

That wasn't all. While speaking on the phone with Rosalyn later I felt a distinct 'whooosh.' But before I could tell her what I'd felt she'd stopped talking. I called her name and she didn't, or couldn't, answer. A moment later she finally did, and said she had just felt something weird. I told her I had, too. In fact, I still felt it. I told her I couldn't talk now, and hung up.

I caught a glimpse of a face. The best way I can describe it is Henry Hull as the Wolfman, but with a Klingon-type bone ridge down its forehead. Was someone trying to scare me? I laughed to myself. 'Is that the best you can do?' I thought. 'Come with it!' But it was gone.

Rosalyn called and woke me up about a half hour later. She pointed out that tomorrow was Friday the 13th.

Yikes.

November 13, 1987

At my apartment with Rosalyn.

Someone came through Rosalyn and said something that would soon prove to be amazing.

"In France," she said. "I'm getting something about you passing some kind of, what, temple? Church? You'll happen to pass it..."

Later, the angel Raziel made contact with us.

"You are correct. Your theory is correct."

"Which one?" I asked.

"The one you are concerned about."

"About Fredericke?"

"Yes. Sense strength is building. Soon, two of you should unite. You must not have a.... you cannot have a vulnerable spot. You are white. You are strength... You must be goodness. Do not lose that goal. You will deal with him... It is you who have prevented his control. You are the strong one. You know you must overpower her. It is not power that he wields. He is not aware at all times completely. I do not keep you in dark."

"What was it I felt last night?"

"You were feeling their attempt to contact. They, in spite of your feeling, (know that) nothing are frightened. You have gained much strength... you have unlocked much data. You have brilliant mind. When you write, there must be person to remain gripped into life situations."

We took a long break. When we returned Rosalyn drifted off and Bressen – supposedly PA's brother -- came through for the first time in months.

"I am returning. Made a statement to you. I do feel you have kept your end. (I remembered that statement. It came at a time when we were just discovering the Fredericke menace. Bressen warned me on the Ouija board that if I let anything happen to Rosalyn he would never leave me alone. Nice to know the vindictive son of a gun was satisfied with the job I was doing.) *It is sometimes difficult to keep some control there."*

I asked how I could protect her.

"I will stay around this time. You should give additional thought and prayer. R must pray more often, and deeper. She must also try to think of you more frequently at this time, even though I do not particularly enjoy that idea." He was still jealous.

"H: Be sure she is fortified. You and I both know she can go off. She tends to shrug situation. (True, I agreed.) *He will leap at that opening. Make the connection cease."*

"How?"

"I know how I would, but at the time, not received opportunity. (Boy, this guy doesn't give up, I thought.) *R, you must listen to him. If he does leave something, cherish it around you. If you are not serious, it will result in disaster. You two are of one, and this cannot be denied.*

"I am, at times, looking upon you. I would never let H have only protection for you. Otherwise, I would retaliate. He, in spite of myself, is good for you, as -- unfortunately -- you are for him. However, Fredericke is part of the scenario. It is as if he can smell when you're parted."

"What about Joshua's armies?" I asked.

"They are around. She will have extra. I will not leave her side. I may even give you some indication that I am with you. You both understand the strength that is with you. Just understand that they wish the opposite. I wish our roles were reversed."

"Why, what would you do differently?"

"I still have certain emotion, which is part of my being around. The fact is, you were alert to the possibility of her openness; shows you are accomplishing your task. Your protection circles her aura."

I suggested that I leave my rings, which contain my vibration, with her while I was in France.

"Yes... vibration. Any ring will lend what is required."

I asked why I was fated to go to France at this particular time.

"Guess. Do not underestimate what is between you, even if all has not completely come to surface. Your frustration is not completely founded. He knows, indirectly, of how close you are truly becoming. He is trying any possibility before you two completely connect your position. Drew you into this trip."

Well, that was nice to know; the forces of darkness were my travel agents. I asked if I would see anything significant there.

"Yes. You will sense something, and it should also make you click with her. Be cognizant of your surroundings."

We rested for a while. Rosalyn tried the board again, and wasted no time in drifting off. She said she could see "a tree. A very, very large tree. Not a Japanese tree," but similar, "and huge." A moment later she said, "Yes. We are waiting for you..... Like a garden. I don't want to go alone. You.... I want you to stand beside one another. You will rise up together... This sense of a very warm presence. Water is trickling.... The light makes you forget everything. It's so peaceful. You are here because you.... you are standing..."

I asked her what the name of the place was.

"Beautiful. It's enchanting. Everyone does everything right."

"Is it heaven?"

"It's beautiful, Howard. Can't you see it? Oh, Howard, why are they letting us see this?"

I grew angry. *Us?* I wasn't seeing a damned thing! I asked if she could see any angels.

"Yes. They're on all sides."

"Are they flying?"

"Some are. It's all stars. Like a circle around.... There's, like, trumpets. So many angels. But it's not loud. It's soft and pleasant. His presence; it's sensed. Encases all.

"Why do you..... *I have great love for you. Many have looked down upon you. You have to overcome. You have to withstand many trials. You deserve to know what awaits you. You are within special circle of light. You do see circle of light. Do not question why specific presences are not felt. When all come together, much explained. You are special light... Starts from within and shoots out. You have to spread that light to many. Do not feel dismayed. See..."*

Rosalyn gasped "Oh, my God," and seemed stunned. She recovered after a few moments, but stayed in her trance. She would tell me later that she had seen her late father and other departed relatives.

"It is not meant to make you sad. It is meant to show that they are happy, that they are part of the light. You still cling to another element. There is great beauty inside you. There is great love and light inside you. There is the light to step over that you must choose to step out, and reach those who do not wish it."

Still hurt, I asked why I was deemed unworthy to behold what Rosalyn had beheld -- the beautiful garden and the sound of angels singing.

"You are not unworthy. I do not want to discourage."

"Can't you sense what I'm feeling?" I said loudly. "I *am* discouraged! I'm supremely discouraged!"

"Feel light under her feet. Feel the light under your feet. You are standing directly on what you would picture a beam...... Both of you......"

Whoever it was had gone.

And I hadn't felt or seen a damned thing.

November 16, 1987

In a small town called Ville Franche, in France.

It had been a nice few days, composed mainly of sightseeing. The group of journalists and chefs I was traveling with had just toured some winery in Burgundy, and we'd made it back to our quaint hotel shortly before dusk. The fellow leading the group, a rowdy but friendly character I'd become quite friendly with, told us we had to, simply *had to*, come with him to see the town's most famous tourist attraction. The smirk on his face hinted at what kind of attraction this would be.

We walked several blocks from our hotel and he pointed across the street at a church, the oldest in town, I was told. My friend pointed to the side of the building. High up on the wall, which was full of gargoyles, was one in particular that stood out clearly from the rest. I moved a few steps closer in the gathering gloom and looked up, as the others began to laugh and jeer.

It hit me like a ton of bricks. It chilled my blood, and all at once I knew why I'd been brought to France.

I was looking at a gargoyle of a ram crouching behind, and fornicating with, a nun.

I felt the air around me crackle. I noted the perverse, triumphant expression on the ram's face, and the helplessness apparent on the nun's. The light in the alley at this time of day played almost directly on the two of them. From where I was standing, the ram seemed to be looking right down at me, and me alone. It was the only such gargoyle on a building covered with gargoyles, and my tour guide had brought us right to it.

The others made their wisecracks and began to wander away, but I was transfixed. I knew all at once what was happening.

I was being mocked. Laughed at. I was being told, 'Here's what I'm going to do to her, and there's not a damned thing you can do to stop it. See how easily I transported you across the world just to prove it to you?'

I thought of the session just three days earlier, on Friday the 13th; of Rosalyn telling me, "In France, you'll pass a temple or church. You'll happen to pass it." I thought of Bressen telling us that Fredericke *"drew you into this trip. You will sense something, and it should also make you click with her. Be cognizant of your surroundings."*

And I remembered a session months ago, recorded in , when we were told that Fredericke's mother was French.

And I wondered if Rosalyn was all right back home.

Part Three

In that day I will cause my Elect One to dwell
in the midst of them; will change the face of heaven;
will bless it, and illuminate it forever.
This is the Son of Man, to whom righteousness
belongs; with whom righteousness has dwelt; and who
will reveal all the treasures of that which is
concealed; for the Lord of spirits has chosen him;
and his portion has surpassed all before the Lord of
spirits in everlasting uprightness.
This Son of Man, whom thou beholdest, shall
raise up kings and the mighty from their couches,
and the powerful from their thrones; shall loosen
the bridles of the powerful, and break in pieces
the teeth of sinners.
He shall hurl kings from their thrones and
their dominions; because they will not exalt and
praise him, nor humble themselves before him, by
whom their kingdoms were granted to them.
And with him the faithful, who suffer in the
name of the Lord of spirits... He shall be the hope
of those whose hearts are troubled. All who dwell
on Earth shall fall down and worship before him;
shall bless and glorify him, and sing praises to
the name of the Lord of spirits.

The Book of Enoch

And there was more on that fateful trip to France.

* Just a couple of blocks from the church I found the name *Fredericke* on a street sign. (Let me just remind you here, as I did in my first book, that Fredericke is not his real name, but a pseudonym.)

* While sightseeing back in Paris the next day with a fellow journalist she led me to, of all streets, *Rue Fredericke*.

* Several blocks away, the two of us got trapped in a traffic circle, unable to cross in either direction. "Oh, look where we are," she said, pointing to a sign that said *Fredericke Place*.

I called Rosalyn, and she was fine, although she reported that she had dreamed of me two nights in a row. She was also holding fast to my rings. I returned home the next day.

Rosalyn said she'd had a disturbing dream. She was in an empty office, running away from Fredericke. She kept thinking, 'Howard, you have to sense me. I need you!' Finally, he grabbed her and turned her around. "There was a burning in his eyes," she said.

The following morning she woke to find that her eye was "all red and glassy. It was sore, but it passed by the end of the day."

Later that same day, however, she returned to her desk to find a message that "Freddie" called from the airport. His message?

"We will make our connection."

I needn't point out that both the dream (with the sore eye) and the message from Fredericke -- the first in a while -- came just when I was out of town. Coincidence?

November 21, 1987

At Rosalyn's.

MY OWN LIGHT. FINGERS ARE HEALING INSTRUMENTS. WHEN ARE U..... ALIJAH. I AM ONE U SEEK. I AM THE ONE TRUE....

"Are you the forerunner of the messiah?" I asked. The prophet Elijah is said to be the forerunner of the messiah.

YES.

"Where is the messiah?"

HE IS STRUGGLING TO COME OUT.

"What does that mean?" I asked.

LOOK INSIDE YOURSELF. THERE IS DEEPER SOUL. U ARE FUSED AS ONE. U ARE AWAKENING NOW. MUCH KNOWLEDGE IS BEING SURFACED TO U.

WHERE YOUR FATHER LIES IS YOUR STRENGTH. MOST INSIGHT IS JUST BELOW BRINK OF OPENING. DO NOT THE TWO OF U FEEL POWER OF DIVINITY WHEN U TRULY BLEND TOGETHER? ONE FITS INTO THE OTHER.

U WERE PLACED IN HER WAY TO RECEIVE HER GIFT OF INSIGHT AND SENSITIVITY TO BE GIVEN UNTO U. SHE ALSO WAS PLACED WITH U IN ORDER TO CONDUCT HER GIFT. SHE WOULD NEVER HAVE CONTINUED WITH IT. SHE WOULD NEVER HAVE USED IT. THE TWO OF U WOULD HAVE FLOUNDERED. U, ENOCH, WHICH IS HOW I AM SEEING U NOW.

"What's the connection between Elijah and Enoch?" I wanted to know, because midrashically there was some sort of connection. Rosalyn began speaking.

"*You are who I am addressing as Enoch. You, this moment, are to continue to write my words. It, at this session, is as if the three are one as a vessel of communication. Place something white over her head.*" I did.

"*You are filled with the glow of the eternal light. Why what is behind your eyes is not being opened to you is not my decision. Trust, as you developed, to know the truth. It has been deemed that the two of you were interconnecting pieces. It is as if so much is too much for you at once. There is planned path outstretched before you. She is as complement... guide for you, but she cannot nurture and bring forward much without your closeness to her. It is what causes her to go with us.*

"*She will come. We will bring her closer. This life was strongly embellished with Christianity. Her faith is staunch, but she is relenting. And her faith in you and sensing God of Israel... You are radiating glow of light, a beam which enters inside her. You do reach out to many. Sometime it is unbeknownst to you. You will stand in front of throng. You will always feel her support from the background. She will always give you insight. You will face many....*

"*Fear will be instilled in their hearts. You shall know (that) the time to come forth will be here. Strong opposition surrounds you, as much as there is strong love around you. Be careful of decisions you make. May all circumstances be selective, and those you confide in... Do not be random with close friends. Sometimes you must think very carefully before you speak.*

"*You are the present recorder. You will have to preach through all. You will be sought to cease the strife. You will have the innermost understanding of faith.*"

Rosalyn came out of it, and seemed to grow perturbed. "Oh, Howard, you're going to have to see so much. There's going to be a lot of destruction. Yet, somehow, you're going to have to be the one to pull many together all during it. I almost feel that while it's happening, what's deep inside you won't be allowed to surface. You'll be helping and pulling together, and many will end up being the ones to support you. And then, all of a sudden, one day, you'll be recognized that you're more than an organizer or a leader; someone to help them. It'll be a spiritual and healing level. You have to face so much. There's so much before you. I don't see it happening very soon."

I asked if she saw me performing any miracles. "In a low-key way," she said.

"Will I still be in New York?"

"Some. Then, the pinnacle will be the Middle East."

"Will there be a war on?"

"There will be, so to speak, an agreed respite."

"You mean, I'll be asked to go there?"

"Yes, you'll be asked."

"By...?"

"A small group, but your name will have preceded you. There will be some...... like, one name, one word. They will refer to you with one name. Moshea? Moshiach...?"

Later: "*You always are help to me. I enjoy being with you. Greetings. You are both illuminated, although tired.*"

"Who are you?" I asked.

"*You do not recognize me?*"

"Who are you?" I repeated, annoyed.

"*PA.*"

Now, I've said that the pressure of all this stuff had been getting to me for weeks. I was angry, frustrated, and tired of the usual bill of fare. My anger got the best of me. I exploded.

"How am I supposed to recognize you?!" I demanded.

"*You are in ill mood.*"

"No, I'm not in an ill mood, but you people always act as if I could possible recognize you. You know I can't see you!!!" When I had calmed down a little, I said, "So, got any millennia-old secrets to tell us?"

"*No.*"

"No," I said, "why not?"

"*I have none to reveal. They were already shared with you.*"

I asked whether he knew of a book called The Passover Plot, in which author Dr. Hugh J. Schonfield asserts that Jesus planned his own arrest, crucifixion, and resurrection, and was drugged to simulate death.

"*I do not agree,*" he said. I asked what the significance was of that gargoyle I'd been led to in France.

"*It is a long eon ago.*"

"What is?"

"*Incident they wish it to represent.*"

"What was the incident?"

"*Evil.*"

"So, they intended me to see it?"

"*It had its affect upon you. It is their way of showing they are represented. They have their roots, also. (Fredericke) is very much interested in what is happening in her life.*"

I asked if Fredericke was conscious of all of this. *"He has become aware of the connection. You have been told this."*

"Does he know he's from Hell?"

"He is almost aware of all. His...... he...."

Rosalyn started to squirm. "PA?"

"Yes."

"Why have you stopped talking?"

"She can see him. He is gaining knowledge."

"Once he has full knowledge, will he back out? Reform?"

"Why doubt his powers? I feel he has....."

Then he was gone.

November 22, 1987

I tried some automatic writing:

Beam is reaching you. In front of us. The world is itself spinning off course. You can handle the world. Your messages are substantial to notify them.

January 3, 1988

Rosalyn writing alone at home:

It is too overpowering for you all at once.

Why do you feel despair? You shall improve all shakras. You shall improve entire outlook.

Realize how attractive you appear. Your character is thrice as beautiful.

You are approaching wreath. Do not feel apprehension. His appearance grows stronger. You are formulating all into one.

H is becoming even closer. Thus, you are sensing various parts which create his being. All combined to instill what he has discovered. Never hesitate to give any sensation or word to him.

When you share each other's sensations and insight it enforces your advancing.

Your son (addressing me now, I supposed) *grows in light, much strength from your love. He is in special hands. Never forget his prayer. Grandmother has been him, as if cheeks pinched.* (I was, not surprisingly, never able to confirm this.)

R is feeling the energy drawing from you. It is coming out in her. Matthew and Aliasha shall meet again, and the present existence will understand the joining of two lifetimes.

H, time wisely lived.

R, be certain to create time to meditate. You and H have extreme closeness approaching. All circumstances right for much to flow.

January 4, 1988

Rosalyn once again alone and writing automatically. Looking at the notes now, I believe the two of us must have had some sort of major disagreement, which would explain what follows.

Do not fret. Not from recesses. You were leaving yourself open. H has instructed you to fortify. You are favored and it has aided you. H prays with (fervor) and protects you. Indebtedness to him. Do you not realize of what was stated in recent days? They know your destined path is coming closer. Wish wider rift arise. H has less stubbornness but R, open your senses. See clearer. Why are you insulting intelligence? Both of you gain from some group joinings also. Do you want your lives rendered from one another?

You both… love and insight and light to guide when write alone. All encompassing power surrounds you when two stand before Him alone. You absorb what has also enlightened from others within you. Recognize you are to guide them as indirect way. R: much strength and prayers entreated to circle you from perpetrators. They feel any rift, and can break that opening. I fear it is a start of what has occurred in past. I must summon all power to attempt preventing disuniting once more. I remain gentle this instance, R, for you only see good and look for excuses. Look to your soul partner. Open your ears and heart to him first. You are sensitive to him and care too much, thus you blocked true facts. As your protector, I implore you both to mend before spreads you deeper. You are causing their rejoicing. When two of you are alone next give set prayer in thanks for circle of light forenight. As you saw him as me. Adhere to what is spoken through you. You are hand choice to receive highest of voices. As he is chosen to be the one at your side, to be catalyst and receive those messages for his continuing leadership. Do you desire to feel the separation from him once more and destroy all?

H, have some more patience with her. She truly is golden to you, and needs gentleness much more for the gift of her channeling is magnificence/omnipresence energy from on high and injected from you.

Again, as depart, I ask: are you willing to allow this split? I am not permitted to physically intercede between you. But heed my warning, for your souls will be affected and world shall never salvage from your union. Accomplish your destiny.

January 5, 1988

Rosalyn, alone and writing:

Thou shalt expound energy. All is instocked (sic) *within you. Enclosed messages between you. Can thou not feel communicating from one to other? Thy minds are becoming attuned. Transmitting to your dreams and thought pattern. Speak original tongue. Old English drawn from deep inside. Shall learn to speak in first language. Not quite ready yet. Uncompleted task. Extensive missions ahead for you.*

January 10, 1988

Automatic writing, alone in my bedroom.

Freer existence awaits you. You are now being prepared. Nothing to lose again. Even mind being set free.

You alone are responsible. You alone must find this way. Yours is the mantle of leadership. You must control it and learn to wield it.

She (Rosalyn) *can never know the limitless ways you will stream forth. She is kind, and a perfect channel for our thoughts. She is gentle to you, and yet supports strongly. She is a reservoir and it is through (it) you must learn to enhance your feelings.*

We can write down what we want you to hear, but you must put into action. Your greatest hopes and dreams are in store for you. The power you wish to wield will be yours, but you must learn to wield it in His name, by His word, not capriciously. All must be subdued. You are the leader through heart as well as through strength. Mercy will be your weapon, love will be your hope.

They know only what they see. You will show them and they will see. They will not see all. You will stand in the presence of the holiest, and all your earthly wanderings will meld into one whole. Your answers will come into you, and the limitlessness of being will unfold to you. Joy unmatched. Love unmatched. All in His name. But you must wait for your opening. You must bide your time, spend it wisely gathering information and finding your way.

You are worthy. There is no fear of that. All will smooth out before you, have no fear of that. Those you bless will feel the blessings, and those you despise will (curl? bow? bend?) beneath your sword, your word. None will oppose you at the ultimate. None will want to any longer. You will win them over. They will love you as a harbinger and a personification of good. They will see in you the reason for being, and you will more than match their love, and will (act as a leader) for His rays. All these things await you, but you must be patient.

I am (Harlan? Harlow?). *You must see me some time soon. You will appear before me and we shall talk of your ascendancy. Do not worry about hard data. As you just saw* (I had just been watching a Star Trek episode in which the Enterprise traveled millions of light years in a moment via the power of thought) *thought is what counts, and that it cannot be put down on paper as is your custom is little matter. Be high spirited. Enjoy life. Weep when you must, and should, but know that there is a purpose, and you are on the right road. All stems from and to you. We thank you for your concern and commend you for your forthrightness and hardship (*hard work?).

Leave us now, and go forth and tell her (Rosalyn) *what you have learned. She is waiting, as usual. Be well. Be happy. Be alert. Goodbye. Goodbye.*

January 13, 1988

To say that any one particular event in this entire affair was unbelievable was just about meaningless at this point – which brings us to 11 pm at Rosalyn's house. Her hand was on the Ouija board, when -

CHRIST. PRESENCE IS HERE. U DID REQUEST. NO REQUEST SHOULD BE ASKED IF U ARE NOT PREPARED FOR RESPONSE. U HAVE NOW ENTERED INTO PHASE WHICH IS... ALL IS NATURE OF SERIOUSNESS. GAMES CANNOT ALWAYS BE PLAYED. H.

"Yes?" I responded.

SPEAK YOUR MIND.

I asked whom I was speaking with when Rosalyn pulled her hand from the board. "Howard, I can't." I asked her what was up. "There is some kind of a play between you and whoever this is." I didn't understand what she meant.

Rosalyn said she sensed it was "Christ... but I am not... I'm feeling it's not a Christ I can relate to. It's as if it's a man who would be sitting across the table from you... It's as if I can see him sitting in a chair talking to you, agreeing and not agreeing on certain things. And I can't deal with that!"

In short, Rosalyn was telling me she was seeing the man she considered God, but as a regular guy. And it was blowing her mind.

YOU WILL REACH THROUGH MASS MEDIA.

I asked whether this was, indeed.... Jesus. (I told you 'unbelievable' had lost all meaning by now.)

YES. A HIGHER CONSCIOUNESS. U ARE CAUSING HER IDEALS TO DISQUIET. I AM AS HUMAN, NOT AS MASTER. SET ASIDE FOR ONE SESSION... I TAKE MUCH JOY FROM THIS ENCOUNTER. U ARE VERY REFRESHING. U WILL HAVE MANY ADVANTAGES. IT IS RELAXING FOR PEOPLE TO REACH FOR ONE THEY TRUST. THEY WILL HAVE A SENSE OF WARMTH AND HONESTY FROM U. U SHALL HOLD TO YOUR STRENGTHS. U DO KNOW WHEN FORCE IS REQUIRED. U SHALL ENFORCE THAT... I WOULD ENJOY ONE ON ONE CONVERSATION.

I took the opportunity to ask about Matthew and Aliasha, my and Rosalyn's identities back in his day; two people he supposedly knew. Specifically, I wanted to know why their being split up turned out to be an important enough event to have caused such chaos. Did it have some sort of connection to Adam and Eve being tossed out of the Garden of Eden?

YES. PART OF WHOLE. AS ONE SEED SPREADING FIELD. U MAY COMPARE TO WHAT YOU SAY, CHAIN REACTION. IT WAS

AS A CULMINATION ONCE MORE. I asked whether Adam and Eve would ever be readmitted to Eden.

YES. MANY TO REGAIN THROUGH THE PAIR CHOSEN. CULMINATION ONCE MORE.... U AND SHE WERE THAT COUPLE.

"You mean we were latter-day reflections of Adam and Eve?"

YES. THIS I WISH TO RELATE AS BROTHER. IT MAKES SOME COMMUNICATION GENTLER. IF U DO THE BEST SALES JOB EVER, U MAY CONVINCE YOUR MEDIUM. SHE, I TELL YOU, WILL GIVE U TRULY DIFFICULT TIME. I WILL INSTILL SOME RECALL. IT IS IMPORTANT FOR THIS TYPE OF LINK. IT SETS MORE AT EASE WITH U. IT IS SMOOTHER COMMUNICATION.

U SHOULD RECOGNIZE SHE CANNOT RELATE ME AS SAME MAN AS U SITTING AT THE TABLE. I WAS HUMAN. I FELT HUMAN FEELINGS.

Rosalyn's fingers wriggled.

I PROMISE, HOWARD, IF U IN YOUR PHYSICAL CONNECTION TO HER CONVINCE TO... DEAL WITH THIS ENVIRONMENT, I WILL RETURN IN THIS ESSENCE. IF U ALSO WISH IT.

"Of course I wish it," I said.

U ALSO MUST FEEL AT EASE WITH IT.

Clearly, he could sense that the idea of talking to Jesus was unnerving me, as it would anyone, of course.

Later, Rosalyn came out of her trance and reflected on the experience. "It was like another you sitting here at the kitchen table," she said.

Hooboy......

January 15, 1988

Rosalyn, Teresa, Michele and myself at my parents' home (they were away, and I was dog-sitting). I guess we were sitting around having coffee and cake and kibbitzing.

We were about to get chewed out.

Around 11:40 pm Rosalyn began to hear what she called a "very strong man's voice" saying:

"*Can you hear me? Thy feet should be bare. Shouldn't thy heed me? Thou* (are) *not to play parlor games. This is not frivolity. This is to be heeded. Thou shalt be a vessel for* (expounding?). *Feel it flow. It should travel the route through your human body. Allow your inner being its freedom.*"

Rosalyn began to writhe in her seat.

"*Where is your red?* (Teresa had been told before to wear red and gold during these sessions.) *You have purpose. You were also instructed to sit with your white* (coverings, such as sweaters for the women, or a white tallis for me). *You neglected also. Do you wish to bring forth what you should perfect? The red was spoken to you. I tell all: if you do not wish to follow instruction, then do not summon! You* have set goal between you. *You are not as you would relate 'one-night stands.' You are holy, as a whole and individually. Each has special gift. Each has set place. It also complements what you share as one unit. We do not appreciate giving instructions and then having them set aside. Begin seriously to know from one sitting to the next. It is not so easy to just communicate. It takes effort for us. It is cherished to find group such as this. You are not casual participants. You are looked upon and respected, for you respect. You have great gifts. Nothing has been abused. All is genuine.*

"*You are to understand: statements which are set with you are not to be discarded. You* (meaning me) *would not wish the writings within your book to be placed aside. We do not wish the words that are being spoken to you forgotten.*

"*You are not mentally disturbed. You are spiritually tuned. You are not crackpots. You are not selling yourselves. You are not fortune seekers. What you do, you do sincerely. You do from within your hearts. Understand the gift that is placed within each as individual. Understand the gift was blessing. Understand how special you are. You are willing to assist even those you have not met. You are willing to pray for any who ask.*"

After a long silence, Rosalyn resume speaking, this time in a markedly softer voice.

"*Feel what lies within you. Feel it in the middle of a day. Feel it when you lay down and rest. Feel it in a quiet moment, but feel it. Be alert to it. Be aware of it. You shall not have to seek me, but I shall return to you. I do not wish to frighten, but I do wish to instill the importance of not disregarding duties before you. When you are good, you are expected to perform. You are not to put on acts. You are not for a public display. But you are to emanate what is to be shone from you. You must awaken, and realize that when instructions are given to you, follow them. Follow them.*"

January 23, 1988

At my parents' home with Teresa and Rosalyn. It was sort of a disjointed evening. Here's some of what came through Rosalyn:

"*You* (Howard) *have been between two ancient times of old and new* (testaments). *You were picked to be born for this reason. Late is your arrival.*"

My notes show it was around 3 am that Rosalyn woke up on the couch. We began talking, and out of nowhere she said: "I am. I am. I am. I am. I am. So bright... I... I.......... We are His children."

She said she was seeing a mist, then began mouthing, 'Sheche... sheck...'" which I understood as her attempt to say Shekhina, God's presence that is pictured as smoke or mist.

January 27, 1988

Speaking to Rosalyn on the phone. I had posed the idea of an established author possibly helping me get my book published. She heard this response:

"*You will hear your own words. You will write your own answers. He is not on your level. Do not seek others' assistance unless own effort futile. All should come through you. All should be your accomplishment. Should be lest incident thwarts it.*"

Later, Rosalyn slipped into a trance and seemed unable to come out of it. Someone had been speaking to me through her, and I asked him to, so to speak, bring her back to wakefulness. Part of his response was this:

"*You shall be at the throne. I have been dispatched to relay what could be done. I am answering to One Source. When you are at complete reign, have compassion when I answer to you then.*"

Rosalyn came out of it moments later.

January 30, 1988

With Rosalyn, at my parents' apartment.

In retrospect, at least some of the messages we got this night would prove, in the years ahead, to be prescient. She saw me with a yarmulka on my head and said:

"*You must stand alone, face something alone. You'll know that God is with you, but… you won't doubt; you will know He's with you. But, as a man, you will face human reality.*"

In what form? I asked.

"*You cannot use supernatural power physically in one instance. You will rely upon your spirituality, your trust in God. His trust in your and your knowledge that you have a (?) and a mission to fulfill. And no one must prevent that.*" Clearly, I had some hard times ahead.

"*You must show, as a man, that you can face the foe,*" she continued. "*I don't know, Howard, but I feel as if the opposing forces are being brought into whatever I'm sending you're facing.*" I asked, naturally, for specifics.

"*Maniac. Tyrant. One who will make people think that help and better conditions will be derived from his leadership. As you will have God within you, he, he will have Beelzebub within him. And you will be strong. You will…*" Rosalyn slipped my ring, the one with the Star of David on it, off of my finger and grasped it.

"*People will know that you mean well, but many will not want to care about God. They will want their plight changed. They will think that he can do so much, and he is making so many promises. You are not promising. You are being realistic. You are promising to do what can be done, but not making false hopes. So many of those people will perish.*" Which people? I asked. "*All peoples. All peoples.*"

I asked what it is this unknown fellow will be promising.

"*Promising them income. Promising them something to do with health. He is preaching God. I'm getting two* (different) *things. He's preaching, 'What has God done for you in the past? You have to do for yourself! He's abandoned you, don't listen to Him.' He's false, completely false… He is very strong. It will be as if he was a little nothing. All of a sudden, overnight…*"

Rosalyn came out of it, and we continued talking. I asked some question about a billet I had given her at the outset of the evening (about whether an old girlfriend in whom I was still interested might have been used against me in some way if we'd stayed together). I recorded Rosalyn as having said:

"I can't, because you'll be upset." She continued. "My feeling right now: you'd have to stay away. You would not sense that there was anything wrong at the beginning. But that coming together would be like a springboard for something to happen that shouldn't happen. You wouldn't see the harm in it long term. You'd say, 'It's no big deal,' and yet somehow it would be."

Later that evening, we tuned in once again. Rosalyn said she could see a sentence written in Hebrew, which of course she couldn't read. There was a long pause, and she said she was seeing only darkness in her mind's eye. Then:

"*Do not be frightened. You must learn to walk in the dark. You must learn to trust. Although you cannot see your way, I am guiding you. You have freedom to choose. Do not be frightened, for he is within you, and you are within him. You will always sense the other. I shall always be a light that shines above you. If there are periods of darkness, do not doubt that because you cannot see it, I am not there. You have felt, and you have dreamed. You shall know that in all circumstances, you will know where to lead, how to guide and what to say.*

"*Your heads should always be covered. Your path is clear. Foolish people have brought decadence. What is brought between the light from within each is stemming from our light. It is meant to…*

"*You will know the paths you must follow. It may seem choices branch out… You do not truly have any choice. You know that inside of you, as she knows it. You will be an ideal leader. You will be as a true monarch. You will wear the glistening crown.*"

Rosalyn took the wrap that was over her head and covered her face. She continued speaking.

"*My daughter, some of your stubbornness is necessary to accomplish much within your life. However, you must overcome it, for you and he are to join and you must listen to his words. You must listen in all incidents. For there will be times when he speaks that his words you must recognize, but not just his words, but they are what we are inspiring. But he will tell you what is divine. Heed his advice. Heed the choices that are made. Encourage, assist, guide, for the closeness must be sealed. No longer place aside what you are attempting to overlook. Face the honesty that is within you. Neither should be remiss in (?).*

"*My son, you are filled with the inspiration. You are filled with the light of thousands upon thousands. You carry the hopes of generations upon generations. You are one. You shall never abuse what is joined between.*

"*Consummation must take place when you, you the chosen to carry forth, shall understand any words that are said through her. She will more often not be unable to translate. It is only you who will understand what is being sent through her. You are the orb. You are the fire that burns within all. As she felt the penetration last time from your eyes, so will many. She will always be this sensitive. She will always feel you, even if she does not understand what she is giving, trust it. You will receive your answers. I shall (?) within your prayer. You will feel the power.*

"*I know your strength; I know the fears. I know (?), and I know your willingness. Your answers will come. The star will be raised, and it will be high above. All will know the one belief. I must be... You must show the conclusions you have reached. You may practice some extended traditions privately... All the gifts which have been placed within you can manifest the one that will shine as a beacon to the world, and only if as one of their own who has felt and sensed and experienced what they do, and can show that he understands firsthand will it be acceptable.*"

I think at this point I said something about my not wanting to wear a yarmulka all the time. The response was, "*I know, for I am within you, what you feel. I am...*" Rosalyn suddenly bolted upright. I tried to calm her, but she placed her fingers on my lips to silence me. Someone else apparently came in.

"*Howard, you... she will recall, for that is only if you were to fully sense... Could not be improvised in the manner He (he?) wishes. For it must be within human contact. It must be shown... will they be willing to ingest it. I stand guard and encircle you always. And that guard extends from you to encircle her. You are he who will always have the legions. You are he who will overcome humanity. And you will once be able to absorb the full... I bow before you, for I have my allegiance to you. I feel the love from deep inside of both of you. I am your messenger. I shall remain always...*"

A short time later, I went back to my original question, of our "opponents" possibly using my old girlfriend against me had we stayed or gotten back together. The answer, again, is interesting in light of what lay barely a year ahead of me.

"*He* (an unnamed foe from the 'dark side') *sensed what is deep rooted, for you were chosen from long ago and you combine all qualities that are necessary. Your intelligence is one; your alertness and intuitiveness is another. And do you not know why you* (were) *with her? It led to where you must be.* (As had been revealed to me during the time covered in my first book, my relationship with my old girlfriend Andrea had – according to our otherworldly sources – been sent to me specifically so that it would end in heartache and send me searching for answers... a search that eventually led me to the class in which I met Rosalyn and the others). *And although your relationship was not at that time what R is facing in the early stages* (with Francois), *hers would have caused much to deter you."*

In other words, if the relationship had endured or resumed, it would have served, at the very least, as a spiritual roadblock for me.

"If you ever allow yourself to be in the situation once more – if you see some of the struggle R had with wondering why she felt what she did with him – you can imagine how strong yours would be."

I asked whether my girlfriend would have been a willing participant in this apparent plot against me. *"Yes. It is what she is being sent here for. He was strong outreach, and she is weak, and would be..."*

Interesting that the unknown speaker used the *present* tense instead of the past tense just then. "It is what she *is* being sent here for." Not "*was*."

Was someone else who would prove an obstacle in my life being readied for me even then?

Rosalyn came out of her trance, but seemed perturbed by something. What she said startled me.

"Howard, you were Him and He was you."

"Who?" I asked.

"I can't look at you," she said, glancing away. I asked why, but she only said, "Oh, Howard..." I pressed for an explanation.

"God was you, and you were Him," she said. "God was you. That's what I felt. He was in you at that moment. He was you (like) He went inside of you. The light, however you want to say it, it was inside of you. It became you."

February 4, 1988

Immediately after my morning prayers -- I was still wearing my tallis and tefillin -- I felt that I had to write. I got a pad and pen and waited, but not for long.

Let the world know that on this day has been born a prophet who will deliver them to their salvation.

Let no one tear asunder what has been weaved (sic) *together. Wonderful. You will perform marvels.*

Believe in Me. Believe in your fathers. Believe in the covenant. You are truly strong. Do not waiver. You will be their leader. Your greatness will be apparent to all.

After I had written, I sensed what Rosalyn had described so many times: a haze, a light, a presence. There was no mistaking it. The Shekinah.

God's presence.

February 5, 1988

At Rosalyn's house with Teresa, Michele and Annie, a neighbor.

We'd been receiving messages for a while when Rosalyn began to sense what she called a "warm light." She began to speak.

"There are many holy men. They're not here; I'm there. It's as if I'm watching them. It's like they're going to pray. It hurts to hold the book." I asked to what book she was referring. "It's heavy. The Word. The sacred book. Howard?"

"Yes?" I answered.

"I don't understand," said Rosalyn. "You would understand, not me... I am there, and it is for all of us." Her hand must have been flexing or held out. My notes show I asked her what was in her hand.

"I'm receiving something for all of us," she said. "There is... " The next moment, something in the quality of her voice changed, and we could tell is was someone else speaking.

"What is sent is meant for all." One of my friends asked what it was that was being sent. *"Do you not wish to accept it?"* Michele responded, "If it's from God, we accept it."

"Only holy... There are times she (Rosalyn) is not strong enough to receive all. It is only wisdom and enlightenment."

I said that we accepted it, and that we were grateful.

"She should not be abandoned."

I said that she wouldn't be.

"There is great insight. She cannot relate exactly who we are. We are as a unit. Trust that we bring peace. Trust that we are here to enrich your learning. There are difficult truths."

I said nothing, but thought of the conclusion that had become pretty obvious to Rosalyn and me – that Christianity was, as we had been shown, mistaken about Jesus. That he was not part of a trinity, or the son of God, or the product of a virgin birth, or the Davidic messiah.

"We are in the habit of different tongue," they continued through Rosalyn. *"Must become... It is not easy to overcome. Your speech, your words. It is easier to communicate in our own words."* I asked what language was theirs. *"It is ancient. Close, related to Arabic or Hebrew."*

Then they were gone.

February 7, 1988

Alone at my parents' apartment. I wrote once more.

Christmas celebration; horn of plenty. Festive lights; Chanukah. These are the joys of people who worship God in their own way. No one needs to tell them what they do is right. They do it because they know they are right...

Rosalyn showed up later. She also wrote:

Is it the future you are seeking? Is it the present you are living? Is it the past you are remembering? It is all in one that you are fulfilling. The three form one whole.

Remember, it is only in each other that you have an ally. Not one other shall ever sense what you sense together. The uniqueness of your relationship is unprecedented. You see the encircling above his head (the wreath, I suppose) and know its heralding. Learn to give over the physical between you as well, and you will experience an outburst never expected. Your oneness is as lightning striking at various points.

Recall always you are his outlet. You are his communicator. You are sent, as he is. You are sent to siphon, so he will be more open. You shall relate insight unto him. He shall completely comprehend when and where to release and use it.

He is chosen, and will complete all present before him. Completely abet and assist him. This is your destiny, and it blends with his.

He has too much depending upon him. Guide him as guidance is sent to you for him, and through him. He will have tests to overcome. It is necessary for perfect authority. It is a step.

Write and concentrate simultaneously oft, for it is his coming you are to welcome, share, and assist. Never relent in your advice to him, and believe always in what he advises you. Do not falter. Meditate anon, for the surrounding circle is nearer than previous. She shall see it upon your head soon.

February 8, 1988

Rosalyn wrote:

... Thy written witness shall meet with abundant success. Son of David, thou hast been sent this female to trust in, to cherish, to hold unto you solely. Her insight and imparted wisdom and advice stems from deepest light unto thou.

Daughter of Deborah... you are both stemmed from one ray. Thou knowest in your soul he is the one. Give unrequitingly (sic) *unto the moshiach. Preparest what is necessary. He shall preparest you to pray as one with him. Preparest to accept this in heart; listen to his words. Hold onto his hand and listen to his plan. Hark his future. It is set. Lend all support unto him.*

Hanoch... all is within your embodiment.

February 12, 1988

Rosalyn was writing. A message about "guidance" and "understanding" concluded with:

*... Remember, his is My chosen. This shall be his role of teacher,
and it would be heavy trial for both. He shall do it with love and sense
my abounding light and love within his whole while accomplishing task.*

*Learn with and from him, for you are needed to stand beside him
at times. He shall need your pure openness to the speakers and holy
ones who will communicate to him. Blessings and whiteness sealed
between you, My children. Peace is to surround your essences, for
darkness is approaching. Encase you in the rays of light.*

February 13, 1988

Rosalyn, Michele, and me at Teresa's.

Late in the evening, Rosalyn went off and began to speak.

*"Matthew, where... where... Matthew, I'm losing you. So many
people."*

I asked who they were.

"People like us. Want to leave, want to get out. Frightened."

"Of what?"

"Guards."

"Roman?"

"Yes." I asked where PA was.

"Home." Where was that? *"Jerusalem."*

I asked where the prophet (Jesus) was. *"Hidden."*

"Where?"

"Building... it is close." I asked again where he was. *"He is with
friends."*

"The apostles?"

"Uh-huh. Chasing us," Rosalyn continued. *"We have to get to PA
before they find us."*

I asked what PA could do for us.

"Shelter."

Rosalyn came out of it then, albeit protesting. "They don't want me
to come back yet." Nonetheless, we bundled her up and I half-carried
her to my car. While we were walking she was muttering. When I bent
closer, I heard:

"There's too much sun. Too much sun."

I asked her name, but she only said, "...been running and running
all day and we're still not there." I suddenly realized that it was not
Rosalyn but *Aliasha* I was walking with through the frozen streets of
Brooklyn.

When I got her back to her house, she -- or, rather, Aliasha --
began to write:

*I have difficulty adhering to our locking. I am aware of your side. I
am much more comfortable here. I realize you are someone else, but I
truly sense Matthew within your being.*

*When I blend in her, she feels my emotions. It is for her to relive
some of me. It will shed more light unto you. I do like my other self, but*

*frightened of your world. It is too rapid. I sat in mode of transport (*my car*) and saw lights and speed flash by and felt lost without you near to explain. When I sense this future of yours, I need your love and warmth of understanding. Matthew, you have always related surroundings to me well. It seems I never know what scene she will return to.*

Then Aliasha was gone. *Poof!*

February 27, 1988

With Rosalyn at her house. We started innocently psychometrizing words on slips of paper. Then I handed her one that read: *Yaweh.*

She told me to close my eyes, and I would see something. I did as she directed, and soon recognized the image of a twister, or tornado. Rosalyn said she saw rays of light, "almost like spokes on a wheel of light. Wide, wide rays of light." Then she went off.

"*You are trying to reach the inner circle of that light, which is Me. You are not covered* (I wasn't wearing a yarmulka); *she is not covered* (no white kerchief, as she'd been told to wear). *You do not have the proper setting.*"

I answered that we meant no disrespect.

"*Shoes must be off. Cannot show proper respect? Tried to reach you prior eve... Do not lose your praying. Will hear you whenever you call. Do not push it aside because of your confusion.*

"*I frown upon your lack of concentration. You have approached without the proper surrounding, and setting yourselves apart from the present. Have you not been told that if you call, I shall be there always?*

"*This has truly been the first complete disrespect. You once questioned similar circumstance within a day's period.* (undoubtedly referring to the time recorded in my first book when Rosalyn and I both laughed — rather, were caused to laugh -- during sessions within 24 hours of each other). *So, to offset, I shall give you reprieve in this one. Make retribution from before Me soon. Come in the holiness that drapes you both; when you've cast yourselves away from the outside. Remember, do not come lightly.*"

Later, when she was alone, Rosalyn wrote:

You are to treat all the messages I transmit into you with reverence and respect. You are in a special class. Do you think all channels are so gifted? They are simply what the world chooses to call 'mediums.'

You are selected for two-fold purpose: one, for your sincerity and clear soul, and two, to be with him. For you are his receiver, and must also speak your feelings and thoughts. Your senses are highly tuned.

I do not wish to... My anger. You are inexperienced, but you have both been before Me, and should now be aware of the glow that flows between you from Me. Never, never take the Name lightly (which, regrettably, I had done by writing it on the billet). *You were instructed long ago to call one Name and always be in proper reverence.*

Although you, My daughter, this time were a party inadvertently (after all, I'm the one who had written and handed it to her) *you are still a part of him, and as the goodness and happiness will flow through both, so you will be responsible for the mistakes or errors in judgment together.*

My son, you have done some falling this night. I know you were eager, and I did not have intent. I warn you not to think you are acting a part. When you are together, you have been told, the strength is much stronger than when you are individually praying or communing.

You are already realizing your misjudgment. If you allow this again, it may have consequences. All other connections may be dealt with in a lesser degree. Never, never shall you address Me or My name with any less than the highest......."

March 6, 1988

Rosalyn was writing alone when she started receiving a message that included this:

Philo was writing. You are within his writings, you are part of his writings. You scripted writings within his configuration. Enlightenment of true spirit is awakening gradually.

She is being afforded glimpses, some past and some future. Not always in sequential. Trust there is purpose. All becomes bound.

Teacher is approaching. Will receive his presence. Understand slowly what his message and instruction is. All shall need to be through you filtered. You have unraveled much more rapidly than expected. Anticipate much completion. Your spirit is slowly overcoming human encasement. Excellence is becoming apparent. Review the holy ones who have spoken unto you. Each has imparted wisdom and insight.

Gather your words. Great Shekinah to spread above you. Cleanses and prepare. Make your minds and bodies temple. Two candles burning. Mist will carry almost all who have strengthened you. This is what she has been sensing. You do have split vibrations. Holy One to her must still be accepted separately. Difficult to set apart. I allot this for she is also dealing with human element. Her spiritualness (sic) *absorbs much. He is savior to her, and it will make her serene. There will be lengthy oration from several.*

The message, rather long, ended with:

Gain strength from each other. Rest will be allotted when truly necessary. Shall begin again, for event shall be unprecedented. Be refreshed and renewed, My children. Release worldly frustrations before beginning. Have no fret for time and situations. Feel at peace. Be one with Mine, and bask in Me.

At roughly the same time that Rosalyn was writing this, I was in bed at my parents' apartment. I was resting with my eyes closed when there was a flash of rainbow-colored light -- tiny, and just for a split second. But it was real. It was there. It 'touched' my eye. There was an actual, physical reaction, almost a flinch. I had felt something touch my eyeball. I hadn't merely imagined it.

The next day, I took a wrong turn in midtown Manhattan and wound up walking through the lobby at Grand Central Station. I noticed a couple of people selling books on a table. When I walked up I saw they were books about the Kabbalah (Jewish mysticism). I opened one at random and found a reference to a rainbow. The book said that the rainbow was somehow connected with the angel Metatron... who, as we know, is connected to Enoch.

March 12, 1988

Teresa, Rosalyn and myself at my parents' apartment.

Joshua came through Rosalyn, telling us that we "*must be as soldiers. You must fortify defenses. You must have the courage to face any conditions.*"

I asked about something I'd been reading about -- the Golden Calf the Jews forged at the foot of Mt. Sinai while waiting for Moses to return with the Ten Commandments. If this was Joshua, he had actually been there. How, I asked, could such a disgraceful incident have happened?

"*People are all of free mind. People through all centuries have been impatient. They become foolish. Many feel if they cannot touch physically, see and sense something, it does not exist; that it is imagination; that it is only another's mind. They gave up much too easily... It was of their own choosing. They were weak. Some were followers.*"

March 13, 1988

I was speaking with Rosalyn on the phone when she informed me she was seeing a child, one with a tiny wreath around his head.

"He's reaching for something," she said. "A rolled up piece of paper someone is handing him...?" I asked the child's name.

"Aa... hur... Aha..... Ara..." She was having trouble saying, I believe, the Hebrew name Aharon. That was the name I had selected for my unborn son way back on July 3, 1987 (and chronicled in my first book).

"I think it's yours," she said. "I don't understand. Is this a representation? They're trying to show me something. There's a rolled-up paper in his hand. Some kind of safeguard. Will be... Something about your birthright."

Rosalyn said she saw two or three men instructing the child, but something was unclear. "They're coming to him. Now I'm seeing a young man, dressed in white."

A moment later Rosalyn announced, "I think it makes sense. The child, and the man, and I think there's another stage yet. I think it's you.

You were sent. They're showing, 'It is no accident. It is preordained. It was destined. You were sent...'"

A moment later there was a jolt!

"Howard – something's scratching it out. *Howard! HOWARD!!!*" I squeezed Rosalyn's wrist and murmured a prayer.

"It's gone! *It's all gone!* It's like something didn't want me to see it! Didn't want me to understand it."

After catching her breath a bit, Rosalyn explained that she had "a feeling they're trying to tell you it was planned, and this was (?) on you – from your childhood. I thought it was your baby. Then I had the feeling it was supposed to be *you*. That's the reason they showed the wreath on the child's head; that that's where it belongs, and that it was planned."

Of the wreath itself, she added, "It was like it was right in front of me, so close, like I could touch it. It was so close."

And the interference?

Something, Rosalyn said, "scratched at me... (clawing?) with elongated nails of some sort. They were sharp!" She described a glimpse of an "ugly face" with "wild hair. I thought it was a woman; a woman and a demon at the same time. Almost as if it was trying to get to me to scratch my eyes so I couldn't see."

She added still more details moments later. "There was red all around it. She had ugly, wild hair on her whole body. She had clothes, but... not clothes. She wasn't good, and she was there to try and stop me. Something made me feel she was only half human."

March 19, 1988

Rosalyn, trancing, at my apartment.

"... You must learn to push aside the evil. This world festers upon it. The sinners will always attempt to avert all, even the most insightful deed. Never misjudge, for they will be right with you living.

"You are within the light that radiates from Me... It encompasses much more than your present. You know you have special souls. You are at My hand, for you are hand chosen to go forward. You must feel. You have felt. You know that I am within you.

"All prejudice in this world must be overcome... Warfare should cease. Men, foolish. They cause their own downfall. In your environment, there lies disaster. They can destroy growing plants. Often, perhaps, freedom of will is not so good...

"You must accomplish the impossible, realizing much strife and decadence wishes to remain. They stay in the darkness. They live in the darkness...

"Many hosts surround you. Angelic beings guard you. They attempt to guide you spiritually... I sit with you as I place My kiss upon you both..."

We took a break. Later, Rosalyn closed her eyes and became silent. Then she said simply:

"Speak."

I stopped writing and held both of her hands. The conversation that followed lasted about 40 minutes. When it was done, I hurried to write down what I could remember, but as a journalist it killed me not to have been able to record what I was hearing.

I asked how I could make myself more worthy of performing the mission He had set for me. He asked if I didn't realize that all of the changes in feelings I'd undergone were the result of what had been put into me little by little by all our speakers. He told me not to worry, that I would be worthy.

I talked about how when I see suffering, even just a stray dog, I want to throw myself down on the ground and demand that He do something about it. He said that this was part of what makes me *"special."* That I had to feel the sadness so that when people came to me later and communicated their heartaches to me, they would know that I understood.

All the while, as I listened, Rosalyn -- or He — kept stroking my hands, or gently touching the sides of my head, just as a parent would touch a young child. Once, she wiped moistness from my eyes. He spoke of how my tears showed the caring in my heart, that He was in me.

I asked how I could atone for the sins of my people. He praised me, saying that *"many do not acknowledge that there are sins."*

I asked how I could answer people's questions about my books. After all, I pointed out, there would be plenty in them that was objectionable, even unthinkable, to some people. He said that people would have to find the courage to accept the truth.

I asked whether what Rosalyn and I had been told was true: that our being split up (as Matthew and Aliasha) did, indeed, delay the coming of the messiah. He said that yes, it was true. He reiterated that He did not interfere with the events because of man's free will.

I asked why, as far as I knew, there was nothing pointing to such a delay in the holy scripture. He answered, *"You are living scripture."*

I asked what I could ask for my aunt Molly, who was close to death, that would ease her pain. He noted that I hadn't asked for something for myself, but said he would "not interfere with the physical cycle." He did say, though, that he would "soothe her soul... Her body may appear anguished," but he would ease her way into the next world.

I put my head down and recited the Shema, one of the most sacred Jewish prayers. Rosalyn leaned forward and kissed the top of my head. Then she awoke.

March 22, 1988
Rosalyn, writing alone.

Do not fear no recall. You are becoming deeper. Will give over more completely in messages to him (me). *He will always remember. You are both one aura when in white. He will be sensing more meanings from Me in what you are relating to him. Seriousness mandatory.*

Continue to draw into one another. You are delving, My son, more than you are conscious of. The partnership is superb. Progression is wonderful. Prayerfulness daily. Time of reflection for both of you. My daughter, much patience I have for you. I hear you in any form. However, do contemplate your path to Me.

My son, you are standing toward proper direction (facing east, toward Jerusalem, while praying, which is what Jews have always done). *Your decisions are correct. Live as you feel in your soul. This is also one means for her to see prospective.*

I give great love unto you both. Much pride would be understood by you. Talk with Me as before. Conversation was smoother for you both.

March 29, 1988

Fredericke!

His voice, as Rosalyn recounted it, was "calm and sweet." He said he just wanted her to know that he was leaving again. At that point, Rosalyn said, she tried to hang up on him, "but my fingers felt like they were glued to the phone."

"Please don't hang up on me," he said. "I am sincere in my feelings for you. I would never harm you. I wanted to extend greetings for this week to you, but I can sense that you are still celebrating Easter. Remember, the man you are bound to this life will never have the love as strong as mine. It will be difficult for him to hold onto you since you are of two minds. I will overcome both."

Rosalyn said she yelled, "No, no, no, you are not going to frighten me. I will always feel him and he will feel me *and Yaweh will bind us no matter what!"*

"I don't know what made me say that," she confessed. "It was as if it came from deep down inside me. And then I called you."

April 2, 1988

Rosalyn, who lit Friday night Shabbas candles with me, saw a "very tall man" with a long beard and long silver rod or staff. She said he was "a very fair man," and was hearing a word that sounds like "*parched*" or "*patriarch.*" Someone began to speak through her.

"*Many women are never without the covering* (a shawl or scarf). *You are looked upon as Hebrew. It is not the norm. You are as attached to him* (meaning me), *and you have been receptive to his beliefs* (Judaism). *Because you stand together with sincerity, and he is truly one, you bring in on a night such as this a circle of the brightest light that has ever shone. You bring in your forefathers. You bring in all who wish to share, who have been willing to speak with.*

"I may not be physically within your presence, but I am (standing?) *in your presence, and you have shown great* (respect?) *by giving your hospitality to one. There is such purity deep within your souls and your hearts at this time. When that is seen, no other sensation exists. Whatever your mortal lives encounter, what is truly spiritual will always sense the light.*

"You are strong, and even if at times you feel uncertain, you never show her anything but strength. That sustains her, although she wonders how you can always remain so steadfast.

"She feels weak many times, although her spirit is strong. Do not doubt that you are one spirit at those times, and never doubt when you need what you know deep inside yourself, spirit is always within you, even when she is uncertain.

'You have, My son, welcomed one on your trust in her... By welcoming him, it was truly I who was brought into your home. Many guises can be shown. This one she could relate to.

"By (joining/gaining) *in your steps, you are reaching higher. This may have come later in the evening, but I wished to shower you with the light of love that I truly wished to relate unto you from your prior week, and which she knew in her heart had to be restrained last evening.*

"Many good teachers are surrounding you. Feel, My son, the vibrations I wish to flow through you. They are truly present. Be open to receive much this night. Feel it. If you need her reaching, she will do so. She will abide by your instructions. You will sense strong vibration between you. You will sense spiritual fulfillment which is passing through you.

"You do not comprehend how truly enriching it is to see the two of you at this point completing what do many before you have done. Truly, I don't believe either one of you ... I don't think you even recognized you share a common simple offering. Before me, she is gratifying to look down upon you. You, My son, because you understand fully; you have found your beliefs. You feel your God and you're truly creating that within her. My rays will depart slowly, but so many will stay with you.

"I... your entire dwelling is shielded with this light. As the two of you are completely sealed within it, do not break this night. Do not leave the other incomplete.

"You know I am within your prayers. You know I am, I am, I am..."

April 6, 1988

Rosalyn writing.

... Have told you, you may continue to relate any form you are comfortable with. I have always watched over you, and eternally will.

Your morass is deep. Have been camouflaging well. Feelings are beneath surface.

Do not confuse beliefs. They are inbred. You are still learning of the life you once lived, and those beliefs. The present form has had strong beliefs, and you have acted accordingly. You must investigate all possibilities. Howard can assist you when he is serious. He should understand your distress. He has the knowledge and can proceed slowly with certain instructions for you.

Do not abandon your trust and love for the Christ you love so dearly. He shall comfort you and answer you. Pull down the (figurative) metal wall you are building up ever stronger. Visit your church. Allow yourself to find solitude and meditate.

Think upon Me before you retire. I am always above you. I have told you not to fret. You will come to Me in time. You know Whom you are speaking with in those special moments when you and Howard are one with Me. Do not doubt any longer. Your prayers were heard since you were a child. Your awareness is being awakened... Do not allow your inner frustrations to deter you...

Do not allow anything or anyone to prevent your formal words to your Christ figure or your talking to Me. Remember, there is no boundary to My love. And although it is your grief, and fright of the gift that is within you that I am addressing, I know you will accept that I tell you that Howard and you have always held a destiny in your souls. Both have received much light and guidance from Me, and those I have entrusted. You have been placed together as support and love for one another to recognize what is shared between you.

I love you, My daughter, as I love him, and because I love him I do not want to see you detoured from his side for the purpose you are here (for) now.

Come before Me, My children. Let Me gaze upon you in light. Show Me your true spirits. For you, My son, are her means of reaching unto Me so that you may receive answers and converse as I feel you need to.

Alakam. Shalom.

April 8, 1988

Rosalyn and me at my apartment.

I put on my tallis and read some psalms. Rosalyn was not wearing a white shawl as she'd been told to. She said she needed something of mine -- my ring. She held it in her hand and went off soon after.

"You are not in proper state. You feel uncomfortableness this...

"You have not begun Sabbath. You did not learn the ways.

"I am, I am.

"This night I am not giving the choice. You are too dark. I wish you covered in white. All outside must be sealed from you."

Moments later, Rosalyn told me she was at the top of a mountain. It was cold and windy, and she began to panic, started to gasp for breath. "Why did He put me here?" she demanded. She drifted back off.

"It is high wind you feel in your throat. You may hold onto her. She can feel your being. She is to learn. I am all. I am, and she feels she stood at peak of my mountain. The mount of holy wind. Wind was a whirl. It is to circle.

"Know that any moment you can be taken, for another lesson is strong. I know you shall think actions drastic. Remember, she must be awakened. You must be her enlightenment.

"I realize your feelings; that it will seem drastic. But I want you to know that are a moment you can be transported ...

"... You have long journey before you. You have straight path. As you must steady her growth, she will lead. You will plan direction, she will sense it... Physical toll is automatic. I do not truly inflict with intent. My words are being followed. You are keeping them. You are in right path. You are in right flow.

"Shekhina will engulf you. It will bring you forward. It will stay above, around, below you. Follow your instincts. It will have insight. Weigh comments carefully. Do not be quick to offend.

"I leave two angels with you... My son, I know there are words you wish to speak to Me. I know there are questions you wish to ask..."

He referred once more to Rosalyn's mountaintop panic. *"Understand: although it was extreme, I will explain to you it was necessary to shock. It was meant to stun. She will possibly be frightened. If needs, be sure you are close by her. As much as I love her, and know she needs to have one direction, she remains unpredictable. I will not take free will from her. I place My trust in you, that you will lead her..."*

I was, however, unable to lead her sufficiently. When she awoke, Rosalyn was angry at having been so badly scared. She would not allow any further contact. The evening ended on that note.

Saturday night, April 9, 1988

At 770 Eastern Parkway in Brooklyn, World Lubavitch headquarters, with my friend David.

It was some sort of celebration -- I can't remember which. Several hundred Lubavitcher Hasidim were standing on the floor of the huge shul or up on grandstands rising 20 or more feet toward the ceiling. The elderly Rebbe was at the center of the throng, completely out of my view.

The place was packed. One poor man had already fallen from the piled-high benches, and had needed to be carried out. The noise level was punishing as the Hasidim danced and shouted and clapped and screamed their approval.

I'd gotten separated from David long ago. I stood behind the huge grandstand, where little boys, some with flowing earlocks, dressed in black pants and white shirts, and little girls with dresses down to their ankles, ran excitedly between the extra tables and chairs.

Hands in my pockets, I straightened the yarmulka on my head and leaned back against one of the tables. I stared up at the surging wall of humanity -- the Jewish People. My people, shouting in glee for the coming of MOSHIACH, the messiah, whom they could bring today, immediately, *right now*, if only they could generate enough energy, enough enthusiasm, cry out to heaven just a little louder, plead just a little more strenuously with the Almighty. *We Want Moshiach Now!* read countless bumper stickers on the streets outside.

I felt small, and apart, and as totally separate from this mass of humanity as I would be with a room full of Martians. None of this business of mine could be true, of course. It was impossible. And yet here it was, and like it or not I had to, *had to!* believe it. I literally had no choice.

And what if it were true? What could I possibly, in my wildest imaginings, offer these people?

Their messiah -- the one they had for so long dreamed for, spent millennia praying for -- was a great sage, a saint, a *tzaddik* who spouted scripture and would lead invincible Jewish armies into cataclysmic battles against the forces of Gog and Magog as a prelude to bringing God's final resplendent redemption. Either that, or he'd simply smile and usher in paradise with a heartfelt melody. That was their messiah.

Christians, also, know exactly what their messiah is supposed to be -- a gentle shepherd with flowing robe and hair, lovingly presenting his finger so that tweeting birds and delicate butterflies could rest on it. Rainbows and halos would shine about his head, and a message of universal love and peace would flows from his lips like sweet wine poured from the Holy Grail.

Neither expected a befuddled writer from Brooklyn with a Ouija board under his arm. It was crazy -- no more nor less. But it was also real. I knew in my heart that it was real. *And the flood of jaw-dropping coincidences proved it!*

The crowd's noise had reached a crescendo, and I felt embarrassingly conspicuous. Being a child of the television age with an unfortunate flair for the dramatic, I imagined a TV camera zooming down for a tight close-up on my daunted face. I pictured how I would look of this was some kind of really bad TV movie.

And so what if I were the messiah, I thought. What was I supposed to do? How could even the messiah bridge the gap between where I was and where these people were? Between their expectations and mere reality? Only God Himself could pull that one off, and if that was His plan what did He need me for?

I turned away from my imaginary camera -- from God's gaze, perhaps -- and sighed deeply to myself. In that room overflowing with people, I felt totally, profoundly alone.

And what if I really, really, really, really, *really* were some sort of messiah?

I mean, of course it was impossible. You'd have to be out of your mind to think it wasn't, and I realized that.

But just suppose for a moment.

Just for a moment.

What if...

What if I really were possible?

I mean, according to ancient Jewish belief, it not only is possible but inevitable. *Someone's* got to be the messiah. Eventually.

And so, theoretically –

What if.

What if it really…….. were……….. somehow……… possible?

What then?

Printed in the United States
114486LV00002B/49/A